P9-DMU-476

CHRISTMAS GIFTS of GOOD TASTE

With these incredible, edible Christmas gifts, you can be the most creative gift-giver in town! This all-new collection is brimming with delicious recipes and charming crafts to surprise everyone on your list. You'll have lots of fun making yummy goodies for loved ones to munch ... zesty snacks to crunch ... delicious drinks to sip ... and tasty tidbits to dip. Consider how much nicer the holiday season will be if you don't have to contend with crowded stores, picked-over selections, and ho-hum gifts that are likely to be returned later. Instead, from the comfort of your own home, share the flavor of Christmas with a batch of snowflake-frosted cinnamon cookies. Or pop in on friends to say "Merry Christmas" with a bag of microwave popcorn seasoning mix. You can't go wrong with our step-by-step recipes, and our easy craft instructions will even guide you in creating festive packaging that's deserving of the mouth-watering morsels inside. Warming hearts and tummies, home-cooked treats and handcrafted keepsakes are a wonderful way to show family and friends how much you care. Have your merriest Christmas ever!

Anne Childs

LEISURE ARTS, INC.
Little Rock, Arkansas

EDITORIAL STAFF

Vice President and Editor-in-Chief: Anne Van Wagner Childs
Executive Director: Sandra Graham Case
Design Director: Patricia Wallenfang Sowers
Test Kitchen Director/Foods Editor: Celia Fahr Harkey, R.D.
Editorial Director: Susan Frantz Wiles
Publications Director: Kristine Anderson Mertes
Creative Art Director: Gloria Bearden

DESIGN

Designers: Polly Tullis Browning, Diana Sanders Cates,
    Cherece Athy Cooper, Cyndi Hansen, Dani Martin,
    Sandra Spotts Ritchie, Billie Steward, Anne Pulliam Stocks,
    and Linda Diehl Tiano
Executive Assistant: Debra Smith
Design Assistant: Melanie Vaughan

FOODS

Assistant Foods Editor: Jane Kenner Prather
Test Kitchen Home Economist: Rose Glass Klein
Test Kitchen Coordinator: Nora Faye Taylor
Test Kitchen Assistants: Brandy Black Alewine,
    Camille T. Alstadt, and Donna Huffner Spencer

TECHNICAL

Managing Editor: Barbara McClintock Vechik
Associate Editor: Candice Treat Murphy
Senior Technical Writer: Theresa Hicks Young
Technical Writers: Jennifer S. Hutchings,
Susan McManus Johnson, and Marley N. Washum
Copy Editor: Susan Frazier

EDITORIAL

Managing Editor: Linda L. Trimble
Senior Associate Editor: Suzie Puckett
Associate Editors: Darla Burdette Kelsay,
    Stacey Robertson Marshall, and Janice Teipen Wojcik
Copy Editor: Terri Leming Davidson

ART

Book/Magazine Graphics Art Director: Diane Thomas
Production Graphics Artists: Mark R. Potter and
    Michael A. Spigner
Color Technician: Mark A. Hawkins
Photography Stylist: Karen Smart Hall
Publishing Systems Administrator: Cynthia M. Lumpkin
Publishing Systems Assistant: Myra S. Means

PROMOTIONS

Managing Editor: Alan Caudle
Associate Editor: Steven M. Cooper
Designer: Dale Rowett
Art Director: Linda Lovette Smart

BUSINESS STAFF

Publisher: Rick Barton
Vice President and General Manager: Thomas L. Carlisle
Vice President, Finance: Tom Siebenmorgen
Vice President, Retail Marketing: Bob Humphrey
Vice President, National Accounts: Pam Stebbins
Retail Marketing Director: Margaret Sweetin
General Merchandise Manager: Cathy Laird
Distribution Director: Rob Thieme
Retail Customer Service Manager: Wanda Price
Print Production Manager: Fred F. Pruss

Copyright© 1999 by Leisure Arts, Inc., 5701 Ranch Drive, Little Rock, Arkansas 72223-9633. All rights reserved. No part of this book may be reproduced in any form or by any means without the prior written permission of the publisher, except for brief quotations in reviews appearing in magazines or newspapers. We have made every effort to ensure that these recipes and instructions are accurate and complete. We cannot, however, be responsible for human error, typographical mistakes, or variations in individual work. Made in the United States of America.

Library of Congress Catalog Number 98-67372
International Standard Book Number 1-57486-146-8

10 9 8 7 6 5 4 3 2

Table of Contents

SIMPLY IRRESISTIBLE

GERMAN CHOCOLATE CHEESECAKE

CRUST

1 1/2 cups chocolate graham cracker crumbs

6 tablespoons butter or margarine, melted

1/4 cup sugar

FILLING

3 packages (8 ounces each) cream cheese, softened

1 1/4 cups sugar

2 tablespoons all-purpose flour

4 eggs

1 package (4 ounces) German baking chocolate, melted

1/4 cup whipping cream

1 teaspoon vanilla extract

TOPPING

3/4 cup sugar

3/4 cup whipping cream

2 egg yolks

6 tablespoons butter or margarine

1 cup flaked coconut

1 cup chopped pecans

Preheat oven to 325 degrees. For crust, combine cracker crumbs, melted butter, and sugar in a small bowl. Firmly press into bottom and 1/2 inch up sides of a lightly greased 9-inch springform pan.

For filling, beat cream cheese and sugar in a large bowl until fluffy. Beat in flour. Beat in eggs, 1 at a time, just until combined. Stir in melted chocolate, whipping cream, and vanilla. Pour over crust. Bake 1 hour or until center is almost set. Cool in pan 1 hour. Loosen and remove sides of pan. Cool completely.

For topping, whisk sugar, whipping cream, and egg yolks in a medium saucepan until well blended. Whisking constantly, add butter and cook over medium heat until mixture is thickened and bubbly. Reduce heat to low; cook 2 minutes longer. Remove from heat and stir in coconut and pecans. Transfer topping to a heat-proof bowl. Let cool 20 minutes or until thick enough to spread on cooled cheesecake. Store in an airtight container in refrigerator.

Yield: about 16 servings

HOLLY CAKE BOX

You will need a 10" square x 4"h cake box, wrapping paper, spray adhesive, craft knife, cutting mat, 2 2/3 yds. of 2 1/2"w wired ribbon, 6" of floral wire, black permanent fine-point marker, and a purchased gift tag.

1. Unfold box. Cut piece from wrapping paper 1" larger on all sides than box. Place paper wrong side up on a flat surface. Apply spray adhesive to outside of box. Center unfolded box adhesive side down on paper; press firmly to secure.
2. Use craft knife to cut paper even with edges of box. If box has slits, use craft knife to cut through slits from inside of box; reassemble box.
3. Place cake in box.
4. Knot a 30" length of ribbon around box. Use remaining ribbon and follow *Making a Bow,* page 121, to make a bow with a 3" center loop, six 7" loops, and two 8" streamers. Wire bow over knot of ribbon on top of box.
5. Use marker to write message on tag.

*T*reat family friends to the temptingly rich flavor of decadent German Chocolate Cheesecake. A crunchy topping — layered over a smooth filling and homemade crust — makes this cheesecake irresistible! Present your gift in a cake box covered with holiday gift wrap and tied with a pretty bow.

BASKET GOURMET

*T*ucked in a basket with a bottle of wine, our Roasted Olive Dip makes a gourmet gift! The creamy dip — a delightful blend of green and Kalamata olives — makes an elegant appetizer served on toasted pita wedges.

ROASTED OLIVE DIP

$1/2$ cup whole stuffed green olives, drained

$1/2$ cup Kalamata olives, drained and pitted

5 tablespoons Greek vinaigrette salad dressing, divided

1 package (8 ounces) cream cheese, softened

$1/2$ cup sour cream

$1/2$ cup mayonnaise

$1/2$ teaspoon Greek seasoning
Toasted pita wedges to serve

Preheat oven to 400 degrees. Combine olives and 4 tablespoons salad dressing in an 8-inch square baking pan. Stirring every 10 minutes, bake olives about 25 minutes or until lightly browned and wrinkled; cool. Drain and coarsely chop olives. In a medium bowl, beat cream cheese, sour cream, and mayonnaise until well blended. Add remaining tablespoon salad dressing and Greek seasoning. Stir in chopped olives. Chill 2 hours to let flavors blend. Serve at room temperature with pita wedges.

Yield: about $2^{1/2}$ cups dip

GOURMET BASKET

You will need $1^{1/3}$ yds. of $2^{1/4}$"w wired ribbon, 10" of floral wire, basket (we used an oval $6^{1/2}$" x 9" wrought-iron basket), hot glue gun, artificial grapevine and berry picks, $2^{1/2}$" x $3^{1/2}$" piece of card stock, hole punch, sheet moss, black permanent fine-point marker, and gold cord.

1. Follow *Making a Bow*, page 121, to make a bow with four 8" loops and two $6^{1/2}$" streamers from ribbon. Use wire to attach bow to basket. Glue grapevine and berry picks to bow and basket. Line basket with moss.
2. For tag, match short edges of card stock and fold in half. Punch hole in corner of tag. Use marker to write message on tag. Use cord to attach tag to gift.

CHRISTMAS CRUNCH

*E*veryone at your next Christmas party will be clamoring for the recipe for our Crunchy Cheese Spread! They'll never believe that chopped sauerkraut, along with green pepper and onion, is what provides the crunch! Be sure to serve the spread in a pretty bowl — and don't forget the crackers.

CRUNCHY CHEESE SPREAD

   2   tubes (6 ounces each) pasteurized process cheese food with jalapeño peppers, at room temperature
   1   package (3 ounces) cream cheese, softened
   1   can (10 ounces) chopped sauerkraut, drained and pressed dry
   1   jar (2 ounces) chopped pimiento, drained
   1/2   cup finely chopped green pepper
   1/4   cup finely chopped onion
         Crackers to serve

In a medium bowl, beat jalapeño cheese and cream cheese until well blended. Stir in sauerkraut, pimiento, green pepper, and onion. Spoon into a serving dish. Cover and store in refrigerator. Serve with crackers.

Yield: about 3 cups cheese spread

HINT OF MINT

*T*he recipient of this thoughtful present will be glad it's a "hard candy Christmas!" Just a hint of mint gives these sweet chocolate pieces their winter-fresh flavor. Stored in a festively decorated dish, this candy will satisfy the most avid sweet tooth.

HINT-OF-MINT HARD CANDY

　2　cups sugar
　1　cup light corn syrup
　$1/2$　cup cocoa
　$1/2$　cup water
　$1/8$　teaspoon salt
　1　tablespoon butter or margarine
　1　teaspoon mint extract

Line a 9 x 13-inch baking pan with aluminum foil, extending foil over ends of pan; grease foil. Butter sides of a heavy large saucepan. Combine sugar, corn syrup, cocoa, water, and salt in pan. Stirring constantly, cook over medium-low heat until sugar dissolves. Using a pastry brush dipped in hot water, wash down any sugar crystals on sides of pan. Attach a candy thermometer to pan, making sure thermometer does not touch bottom of pan. Increase heat to medium and bring to a boil. Cook, without stirring, until mixture reaches soft-crack stage (approximately 270 to 290 degrees). Test about $1/2$ teaspoon mixture in ice water. Mixture will form hard threads in ice water but will soften when removed from water. Remove from heat and stir in butter and mint extract. Pour into prepared pan. Let candy harden.

Use ends of foil to lift candy from pan. Break into pieces. Store in an airtight container.

Yield: about 1 pound, 7 ounces candy

ELEGANT EDIBLES

*O*ur *Gourmet Almonds
will delight even the most
discriminating of tastes. A
glaze of coffee-flavored liqueur,
cocoa, and cinnamon makes
the nuts a delectable treat! Dazzle
the recipient by wrapping the
treats in a gold gift box tied
with ribbon, tassels, and
small baubles.*

GOURMET ALMONDS

  1 egg white
  2 tablespoons coffee-flavored
      liqueur
  3 cups whole almonds
      (about 1 pound)
$1/2$ cup superfine sugar
  2 tablespoons cocoa
  1 teaspoon ground cinnamon
$1/4$ teaspoon salt

Preheat oven to 225 degrees. Combine
egg white and liqueur in a medium bowl;
beat until foamy. Stir in almonds. In a
small bowl, combine sugar, cocoa,
cinnamon, and salt. Stir sugar mixture
into almond mixture. Spread almonds on
a lightly greased baking sheet. Bake
1 hour, stirring every 15 minutes. Cool
on baking sheet on a wire rack. Store
almonds in an airtight container.

Yield: about $4^{1}/_{4}$ cups almonds

FABULOUS FRUIT SPREADS

*G*ive friends a taste
*of the tropics with these bagel
spread mixes. The fruity blends
are created in a flash by
mixing gelatin and dried fruit.
Simply combine with cream
cheese and enjoy! To make the
nifty packets, fuse fabric to a
paper bag, draw on "stitches,"
and tie on snowman spreaders
for wintry fun.*

FRUITY BAGEL SPREAD MIXES

*Try variations of these mixes using your
favorite gelatin and dried fruit.*

VERY BERRY MIX
   1 package (3 ounces) raspberry
       gelatin
  ¹/2 cup dried sweetened cranberries

In a small bowl, combine gelatin and
dried fruit. Store in a resealable plastic
bag in refrigerator. Give with serving
instructions.

Yield: about ³/4 cup mix

TROPICAL FRUIT MIX
   1 package (3 ounces) pineapple
       gelatin
  ¹/2 cup chopped dried pineapple
  ¹/4 cup flaked coconut

In a small bowl, combine gelatin, dried
fruit, and coconut. Store in a resealable
plastic bag in refrigerator. Give with
serving instructions.

Yield: about 1 cup mix

To serve: In a small bowl, beat
3 tablespoons mix into one 8-ounce
package softened cream cheese until
well blended. Cover and chill 2 hours to
let flavors blend. Serve spread on bagels.

Yield: about 1 cup spread

BAGEL MIX GIFT BAGS

For each bag, you will need a 4" x 7¹/2"
brown paper bag, hot glue gun, fabric,
paper-backed fusible web, permanent
medium-point black marker, several 18"
lengths of red raffia, and a decorative
spreader.

1. Leaving bag folded, glue bottom to
secure.
2. Measure height and width of bag;
subtract ¹/4" from each measurement.
Follow *Making Appliqués*, page 121, to
make one appliqué using the determined
measurements. Fuse appliqué to front of
bag.
3. Fold top of bag 2" to front. Use marker
to draw "stitches" along sides and bottom
of flap.
4. Place bagel spread mix and serving
instructions in bag. Knot several lengths of
raffia around bag. Tie raffia ends into a
bow around spreader.

PIMIENTO PIZZAZZ

*S*imple to prepare and packed with flavor, this gourmet cheese spread makes an ideal last-minute gift. No one will guess that you created the zesty mixture using only three ingredients! Delivery is easy, too — just dress up a brown bag with paint and a Christmas card.

GOURMET PIMIENTO CHEESE SPREAD

1   container (14 ounces) pimiento cheese spread
1   cup finely chopped pecans, toasted
1/2   cup dill pickle relish *or* 1/4 cup sweet pickle relish
    Crackers to serve

In a medium bowl, combine cheese spread, pecans, and relish. Stir until well blended. Cover and chill 2 hours to let flavors blend. Serve with crackers.

Yield: about 21/4 cups spread

BROWN BAG WITH CHRISTMAS CARD MOTIF

You will need a Christmas card, craft glue, lunch-size brown paper bag, white and gold acrylic paint, paintbrush, 11/4"w wooden star, hole punch, green raffia, and a hot glue gun.

1. Cut desired motif from card. Use craft glue to glue card to front of bag; allow to dry.
2. Paint white dots on bag; paint wooden star gold. Allow to dry.

3. Place gift in bag. Fold top of bag 11/2" to back. Punch two holes 1" apart in center of folded portion of bag.

4. Thread several 15" lengths of raffia through holes and tie into a bow at front of bag. Hot glue star to knot of bow.

OVERNIGHT SENSATION

*S*end caring thoughts
with a gift that the family can
enjoy together. Overnight Ham-
and-Egg Casserole is ready to
bake, so Mom can spend less
time in the kitchen and more
time around the tree on
Christmas morning. Deliver
the hearty dish in a covered
baking pan that's tied with
ribbon. Be sure to include
the baking instructions!

OVERNIGHT HAM-AND-EGG CASSEROLE

8	slices Texas-style (thick-slice) bread, cut into 1-inch cubes
2¼	cups cubed smoked ham (about 1 pound)
2	cups (8 ounces) shredded Cheddar cheese, divided
12	eggs, beaten
3	cups half and half
¼	cup chopped fresh parsley
1	teaspoon salt
1	teaspoon dry mustard
½	teaspoon garlic powder
½	teaspoon ground black pepper
¼	teaspoon paprika to garnish

Layer half of bread cubes in a greased 9 x 13-inch baking dish. Sprinkle half of ham and 1 cup cheese over bread. Layer remaining bread and ham. In a large bowl, combine eggs, half and half, parsley, salt, dry mustard, garlic powder, and pepper. Beat until well blended. Pour egg mixture over ham and bread. Sprinkle with remaining 1 cup cheese and paprika. Cover and chill overnight. Give with baking instructions.

Yield: 8 to 10 servings

To bake: Remove casserole from refrigerator and let stand 30 minutes before baking. Bake uncovered in a 350-degree oven 50 to 60 minutes or until a knife inserted in center comes out clean. Serve warm.

BERIBBONED BAKING DISH

You will need spray adhesive, one 8¼" x 12½" piece each of fabric and poster board, double-sided tape, 9" x 13" baking dish with lid, 2½ yds. of 1½"w ribbon, self-adhesive gift tag, white card stock, decorative-edge craft scissors, hole punch, and 12" of gold cord.

1. Apply spray adhesive to wrong side of fabric; smooth fabric onto poster board. Round corners of fabric-covered poster board and use tape to attach poster board to lid.
2. Place lid on casserole dish. Beginning with center of ribbon across top of dish, wrap ribbon to bottom. Twist ribbon at bottom and bring ends to top of dish. Tie ribbon ends into a bow.
3. For tag, apply gift tag to card stock. Leaving a ¼" card stock border, use craft scissors to cut out tag. Punch hole in corner of tag. Use cord to attach tag to ribbon.

MORNING BOOST

*S*tart that special someone's day off with an eye-opening breakfast treat. Ideal for the coffee amorist, our Cappuccino Waffle Mix with Coffee Syrup is sure to provide a morning boost. A decorated lunch bag filled with waffle mix and accompanied by a bottle of syrup can be given in a plastic crate that will come in handy later. Be sure to send along the serving instructions!

CAPPUCCINO WAFFLE MIX WITH COFFEE SYRUP

CAPPUCCINO WAFFLES

- 1/2 cup butter or margarine, softened
- 1 cup sugar
- 1 teaspoon vanilla extract
- 1 1/3 cups all-purpose flour
- 1/3 cup nonfat dry milk
- 1/4 cup non-dairy powdered creamer
- 2 tablespoons instant coffee granules
- 2 teaspoons baking powder
- 1/4 teaspoon salt
- 1/4 teaspoon ground cinnamon

COFFEE SYRUP

- 1 cup strongly brewed coffee
- 2 cups sugar

For cappuccino waffles, cream butter, sugar, and vanilla in a medium bowl until fluffy. In a small bowl, combine remaining ingredients. On low speed of an electric mixer, beat dry ingredients into creamed mixture (mixture will be crumbly). Transfer to a resealable plastic bag; store in refrigerator. Give with serving instructions.

For coffee syrup, combine coffee and sugar in a heavy medium saucepan. Stirring constantly over medium-high heat, cook mixture until sugar dissolves. Without stirring, bring mixture to a boil; boil 2 minutes. Remove from heat; cool to room temperature. Store in an airtight container in refrigerator.

Yield: about 4 cups waffle mix and 1 3/4 cups syrup

To serve: Preheat waffle iron. Transfer bag of waffle mix into a medium bowl. Add 3/4 cup water and 2 eggs; stir just until blended. For each waffle, pour about 2/3 cup batter into waffle iron. Bake 3 to 5 minutes or according to manufacturer's instructions. Serve hot waffles with coffee syrup.

Yield: about five 8-inch waffles

BREAKFAST GIFT BAG

You will need silver spray paint, lunch-size white paper bag, craft glue, Christmas card, hole punch, and red and green 1/4"w curling ribbons.

1. Spray paint front of bag silver; allow to dry.
2. Glue Christmas card to front of bag; allow to dry. Place gift in bag.
3. Fold top of bag 1" to front twice. Punch two holes 1" apart in center of folded portion of bag.
4. Thread ribbons through holes and tie into a bow at front of bag. Curl ribbon ends.

STIRRING UP FUN

*S*tir up some holiday fun
with a bundle of Chocolate-
Cinnamon Stirrers. These
flavorful spoons can be used
to sweeten coffee or cocoa.
A whimsical cross-stitched mug
insert and a festive plaid bow
add seasonal flair to the offering.

CHOCOLATE-CINNAMON STIRRERS

*Spoons should be given the day they're
made.*

> Vegetable oil cooking spray
> 4 ounces chocolate candy coating,
>   chopped
> 2 ounces semisweet baking
>   chocolate
> 1/4 teaspoon cinnamon-flavored oil
>   (used in candy making)
> Red and green heavyweight plastic
>   spoons
> Miniature marshmallows

Line a jellyroll pan with waxed paper;
spray with cooking spray. Combine candy
coating, chocolate, and oil in top of a
double boiler. Place over simmering water
until chocolate softens; stir until smooth.
Dip spoons into chocolate, filling bowls of
spoons. Wipe excess chocolate from
bottoms of spoons. Place spoons on
prepared pan with handles on rim and
spoons level. Place marshmallows on
chocolate. Allow chocolate to harden.
Wrap spoons individually. Use spoons to
stir coffee or hot chocolate.

Yield: about 10 spoons

SNOWMAN CROSS STITCH MUG

You will need a Vinyl Weave™ mug insert
(14 ct), embroidery floss (see color key,
page 102), red Mugs Your Way™ mug,
clear cellophane bag, and 22" of 1 1/2"w
wired ribbon.

*Refer to Cross Stitch, page 123, before
beginning project.*

1. Matching short edges, fold insert in half
to find center; unfold. Using three strands
of floss for *Cross Stitch* and one strand of
floss for *Backstitch*, center and stitch
design, page 102, on right half of insert.
2. Follow manufacturer's instructions to
secure stitched insert in mug.
3. Place stirrers in cellophane bag. Tie
ribbon into a bow around top of bag.
Place bag in mug.

A FRESH IDEA

A light alternative to sweets, a basket full of fresh fruit can be as enjoyable as a calorie-laden dessert when you include a jar of our Honey-Lemon Fruit Dressing. The creamy dip blends up quickly, and it's ideal for your health-conscious pals. Dress up the basket with a starry bow and tag for delivery.

HONEY-LEMON FRUIT DRESSING

For best consistency, use yogurt with 2% or higher milkfat content.

    1 package (3 ounces) cream cheese, softened
    1 tablespoon honey
  1/3 cup firmly packed brown sugar
  1/2 teaspoon vanilla extract
    1 container (8 ounces) custard-style lemon yogurt (2% or higher milkfat)
       Fresh fruit to serve

In a small bowl, beat cream cheese and honey until fluffy. Add brown sugar and vanilla; beat until well blended. Stir in yogurt. Store in an airtight container in refrigerator. Serve with fresh fruit.

Yield: about 1 1/2 cups dressing

STAR RIBBON BASKET

You will need a household sponge, green acrylic paint, basket (we used a 9" x 12" oval basket with handle), 2 1/2"w wired ribbon, 6" of floral wire, pint-size canning jar with lid and band, tracing paper,

yellow card stock, and a black permanent fine-point marker.

1. Follow *Sponge Painting,* page 122, to lightly sponge paint basket green; allow to dry.
2. Measure around basket; add 2". Cut a length of ribbon the determined measurement. With knot at one side of handle, knot ribbon around basket.
3. Using ribbon, follow *Making a Bow,* page 121, to make a bow with four 6" loops, a center loop, and two 7" streamers. Thread one wire end on bow through ribbon knot; wire bow to handle.
4. For jar lid cover, cut 9" from ribbon; notch ends. Center ribbon over lid; place band on jar.
5. For tag, trace pattern, page 102, onto tracing paper; cut out. Using pattern, cut tag from card stock. Use marker to draw "stitches" along edges of tag and write message.

HOMESTYLE RELISH

Here's a great gift that's quick to make. Simply chop store-bought bread and butter pickles in a food processor and then combine them with celery, onion, green pepper, and cauliflower. The result — a hearty relish packed full of flavor! Wrap a pickle jar with cardboard and fabric for a homestyle delivery.

BREAD AND BUTTER PICKLE RELISH

- 2 jars (16 ounces each) bread and butter pickle slices
- 1 cup small cauliflowerets
- ½ cup chopped celery
- ½ cup chopped green pepper
- ¼ cup chopped onion
- ½ teaspoon celery seed
- ½ teaspoon ground turmeric

Drain pickles, reserving jars and 1¼ cups juice. Process pickles in a food processor until finely chopped; drain. In a large bowl, combine pickles, cauliflowerets, celery, green pepper, onion, celery seed, turmeric, and reserved pickle juice. Spoon into reserved jars. Cover and store in refrigerator.

Yield: about 4 cups relish

PLAID PICKLE JAR

You will need a jar with lid, fabric, craft glue, corrugated craft cardboard, hot glue gun, natural raffia, and one ½" dia. button.

1. Draw around lid on wrong side of fabric; cut out circle ¼" inside drawn line. Glue circle to lid; allow to dry.
2. Measure around jar; add ½". Cut a piece from cardboard 2½"w by the determined measurement, and a piece from fabric 1½"w by the determined from measurement. Using craft glue, center and glue fabric piece on cardboard; allow to dry.
3. Hot glue cardboard around jar.
4. Tie several lengths of raffia into a bow around jar. Hot glue button to knot of bow.

Loaves of Rye and White Swirl Bread are ideal gifts to give to your circle of friends. The colorful swirl pattern reflects the harmony that creates lasting relationships. For a gift with practical appeal, sponge paint a trio of Christmas trees on a handy canvas tote and top with ribbon bows.

RYE AND WHITE SWIRL BREAD

2	packages dry yeast
2¼	cups warm water
4½	cups all-purpose flour, divided
2	tablespoons sugar
1	teaspoon salt
¼	cup vegetable oil
3	tablespoons molasses
1½	tablespoons cocoa
1½	cups rye flour
	Vegetable oil cooking spray
1	egg
1	teaspoon water
1	tablespoon butter or margarine, melted

In a small bowl, dissolve yeast in 2¼ cups warm water. In a large bowl, combine 3 cups all-purpose flour, sugar, and salt. Add oil and yeast mixture to dry ingredients; stir until well blended. Place half of dough in another large bowl.

Add molasses and cocoa to first bowl. Gradually add rye flour; stir until a soft dough forms. Turn rye dough onto a lightly floured surface and knead about 5 minutes or until dough becomes smooth and elastic. Place in a large bowl sprayed with cooking spray, turning once to coat top of dough.

Add remaining 1½ cups all-purpose flour to second bowl; stir until a soft dough forms. Turn white dough onto a lightly floured surface and knead about 5 minutes or until dough becomes smooth and elastic. Place in a large bowl sprayed with cooking spray, turning once to coat top of dough. Cover both bowls and let rise in a warm place (80 to 85 degrees) 1¼ hours or until doubled in size.

Turn rye and white doughs separately onto a lightly floured surface and punch down. Divide each dough in half. Using a floured rolling pin, roll half of white dough into a 10-inch square. Roll half of rye dough into a 9-inch square. Brush any surface flour from dough. In a small bowl, beat egg and 1 teaspoon water until foamy. Brush egg mixture on top of white square. Place rye square on white square. Brush egg mixture on top of rye square. Roll up dough tightly. Pinch ends to seal dough. Place dough, seam side down, in a greased 5 x 9-inch loaf pan. Spray top of dough with cooking spray, cover, and let rise in a warm place 1 hour or until doubled in size. Repeat with remaining white and rye dough.

Preheat oven to 350 degrees. Bake 28 to 32 minutes or until bread is golden brown and sounds hollow when tapped. Remove from pans. Brush tops of loaves with butter. Serve warm or cool completely. Store in an airtight container.

Yield: 2 loaves bread

TREE TOTE BAG

You will need tracing paper, compressed craft sponge, green acrylic paint, canvas bag (we used a 6" x 9½" canvas bag with handles), brown medium-point permanent marker, red dimensional paint, three 7" lengths of ³/₈"w ribbon, hot glue gun, and tissue paper.

1. Trace pattern, page 102, onto tracing paper; cut out. Using pattern, cut shape from sponge.
2. Refer to *Sponge Painting,* page 122, to sponge paint trees on bag; allow to dry.
3. Use marker to draw tree trunks. Use red paint to decorate trees. Allow to dry.
4. Tie each ribbon length into a bow. Glue one bow to each tree top.
5. Line bag with tissue paper; place gift in bag.

ANY WAY YOU SLICE IT

No matter how you slice it, our Peachy Pizza Dessert offers a fun ending for a holiday meal. The fruity delicacy starts with a cake mix "crust" topped with canned peaches. Slide the mouth-watering masterpiece into a decorated take-out box for delivery.

PEACHY PIZZA DESSERT

  1 package (18¼ ounces) white cake mix
1¼ cups quick-cooking oats, divided
  ½ cup butter or margarine, softened and divided
  1 egg
  ⅓ cup firmly packed brown sugar
  ¼ teaspoon ground mace
  ¼ teaspoon ground cinnamon
  ½ cup chopped slivered almonds, toasted
  2 cans (15¼ ounces each) peach halves in heavy syrup, drained and cut into thin slices

Preheat oven to 350 degrees. In a large bowl, combine cake mix, 1 cup oats, and 6 tablespoons butter. Beat at low speed of an electric mixer until well blended. Reserve 1 cup of crumb mixture in a medium bowl. Stir egg into remaining crumb mixture. Press into a greased 12-inch-diameter pizza pan. Bake 15 minutes or until edges are lightly browned. Add remaining ¼ cup oats, brown sugar, mace, cinnamon, and remaining 2 tablespoons butter to reserved crumb mixture. Beat with mixer until well blended. Stir in almonds. Place peach slices over baked crust. Sprinkle with crumb mixture. Bake 20 to

25 minutes or until top is golden brown. Serve warm or at room temperature. Store in an airtight container in refrigerator.

Yield: about 12 servings

PIZZA BOX

You will need wrapping paper, poster board, 14½" square pizza box, spray adhesive, craft glue, two 42" lengths of ⅞"w wired ribbon, 8" of floral wire, hot glue gun, artificial greenery (we used a pine branch and holly leaves with berries), and an artificial peach with leaves.

1. Cut a piece from wrapping paper and poster board to fit top and each side of box.
2. Apply spray adhesive to wrong side of paper pieces; smooth onto poster board pieces. Use craft glue to glue poster board pieces to box; allow to dry.
3. Place dessert in box. Knot one ribbon length around box. Using remaining ribbon, follow *Making a Bow*, page 121, to make a bow with six 5" loops and two 4" streamers. Use wire to attach bow to knot of first ribbon.
4. Hot glue greenery and fruit to bow.

ANGELIC SNACKS

*P*resented in a package adorned with angels, our *Heavenly Snack Mix* is a thoughtful way to acknowledge the special people in your life. The mixture of cereal, pretzels, and nuts is coated with brown sugar and honey. A dusting of confectioners sugar offers a heavenly finish.

HEAVENLY SNACK MIX

- 3 cups square rice cereal
- 3 cups round oat cereal
- 2 cups small pretzel twists
- 1 can (6 ounces) whole almonds
- 3/4 cup firmly packed brown sugar
- 6 tablespoons butter or margarine
- 3 tablespoons honey
- 1/8 teaspoon salt
- 1 teaspoon vanilla extract
- 1/4 teaspoon baking soda
  Confectioners sugar

Preheat oven to 250 degrees. In a large greased roasting pan, combine cereals, pretzels, and almonds. Combine brown sugar, butter, honey, and salt in a medium saucepan over medium heat. Stirring constantly, bring to a boil; boil 1 minute. Remove from heat; stir in vanilla and baking soda. Pour over cereal mixture; stir until coated. Bake 45 minutes, stirring every 15 minutes. Transfer to a very large bowl. Sprinkle confectioners sugar over warm mixture; toss to coat thoroughly. Let cool. Store in an airtight container.

Yield: about 11 cups snack mix

ANGEL SNACK BAG

You will need a 3 1/2" x 7" cellophane bag, 12" of 1 1/2"w ribbon, angel-motif gift box, gold permanent fine-point marker, 1 3/4" x 2 1/2" piece of ecru card stock, hole punch, and 5" of gold cord.

1. Place gift in bag. Tie ribbon into a bow around top of bag.

2. Place bag in box.

3. For tag, use marker to write message on card stock. Punch hole in tag. Use cord to attach tag to gift.

HOMER'S AWARD-WINNING FRUITCAKE

This prize-winning fruitcake recipe, contributed by a state-fair blue-ribbon winner, will put you in first place with folks on your gift list. The traditional Christmas offering is a cornucopia of tasty ingredients, from candied fruit and cherries to crunchy pecans and walnuts. One batch makes plenty of miniature cakes for sharing.

HOMER'S AWARD-WINNING FRUITCAKE

This fruitcake, made by Homer Rogers of Little Rock, won "Best of Show in Cakes" at the 1998 Arkansas State Fair and Livestock Show.

   2½ cups pecan halves
   1 container (16 ounces) diced
      mixed candied fruit
   1 container (16 ounces) glazed
      pineapple
   1½ cups chopped walnuts
   1 container (8 ounces) red candied
      cherries
   1 container (8 ounces) green
      candied cherries
   1 package (8 ounces) chopped dates
   1 container (4 ounces) diced
      candied orange peel
   1 container (4 ounces) diced candied
      lemon peel
   1 cup water
   3½ cups all-purpose flour, divided
   2 cups butter or margarine, softened
   1½ cups sugar
   ½ cup corn syrup
   6 eggs
   1 teaspoon salt
   1 cup corn syrup for glaze

Preheat oven to 300 degrees. Grease a 6-mold fluted tube pan; set aside. In a large bowl, combine pecans, mixed fruit, pineapple, walnuts, cherries, dates, orange peel, lemon peel, and water. Stirring frequently, let stand 10 minutes or until water is absorbed. Add 2 cups flour; and stir until fruit and nuts are evenly coated. In another large bowl, beat butter, sugar, and ½ cup corn syrup until fluffy. Add eggs, salt, and remaining 1½ cups flour; beat until well blended. Stir fruit mixture into batter until well blended. Spoon batter into pan, packing down to avoid air pockets and completely filling molds. Bake 50 to 60 minutes or until a toothpick inserted in center of cake comes out clean. Cool in pan 10 minutes. Remove from pan and cool completely on a wire rack. Repeat using remaining batter for each batch of cakes. Store in an airtight container.

For glaze, bring 1 cup corn syrup to a boil in a small saucepan over medium heat; boil 1 minute. Brush hot syrup over top and sides of cakes. Store in an airtight container.

Yield: about 15 small cakes

HOMER'S FRUITCAKE BASKET

You will need a basket (we used a 5" dia. basket), 1"w ribbon, hot glue gun, artificial greenery garland (we used a garland with miniature holly leaves and berries), ecru and green card stock, decorative-edge craft scissors, craft glue, black permanent fine-point marker, hole punch, and gold cord.

1. Measure around rim of basket; add 18". Cut a length of ribbon the determined measurement. Tie into a bow around rim of basket. Hot glue greenery to ribbon.
2. For tag, cut a 2¼" x 3¾" piece from green card stock. Using craft scissors, cut a 2¼" x 3¾" piece from ecru card stock. Glue ecru piece to green piece. Glue two leaves from greenery to corner of tag; allow to dry. Use marker to write message on tag. Punch hole in corner of tag. Use cord to attach tag to bow.

COLORFUL CRUNCH

A colorful addition to any relish tray, Red Onion Pickles combine the sweet, tangy flavor of red onions with the spicy goodness of red chili pepper and garlic. The crunchy condiment makes a thoughtful little hostess gift! Our "Noel" bag makes it easy to take along a fabric-topped jar of the pickles.

RED ONION PICKLES

- 1 tablespoon pickling spice
- 1 clove garlic, halved
- 1 small dried red chili pepper
- 1 quart white wine vinegar
- 2 cups sugar
- 1/2 teaspoon salt
- 1 sprig fresh rosemary
- 3 pounds red onions, sliced into 1/4-inch slices and separated into rings

Place pickling spice, garlic, and chili pepper in several layers of cheesecloth; tie into a bundle with kitchen twine. In a large Dutch oven, combine vinegar, sugar, salt, and rosemary. Add spice bundle. Bring to a boil over medium-high heat. Reduce heat to medium; cover and simmer 5 minutes. Stir in onions; continue to simmer 5 minutes, stirring constantly. Discard spice bundle and rosemary sprig. Spoon onion mixture into heat-resistant jars; cover and cool to room temperature. Store in refrigerator.

Yield: about 10 cups pickles

"NOEL" BAG AND JAR LID COVER

You will need fabric, paper-backed fusible web, 7" x 9" brown paper gift bag, colored pencils, photocopy of label (page 104) on white card stock, spray adhesive, hot glue gun, one 3/4" dia. and four 5/8" dia. buttons, jar with lid, pinking shears, rubber band, and red and natural raffia.

1. Follow *Making Appliqués*, page 121, to make one 6" square appliqué from fabric; fuse to front of bag.

2. Use colored pencils to color label. Cut out label. Apply spray adhesive to wrong side of label; center and smooth label onto appliqué. Glue one 5/8" dia. button to each corner of label.

3. For jar lid cover, draw around lid on wrong side of fabric. Using pinking shears, cut out circle 3" outside drawn line. Center circle over lid; secure with rubber band. Tie several lengths of raffia into a bow around jar, covering rubber band. Glue 3/4" dia. button to knot of bow.

THIS IS ONE HOT GIFT!

*T*he spicy design that adorns our *Jalapeño Snack Mix* packages promises that this is one hot gift! To make it, simply pour a zesty combination of butter, peppers, and spices over some of your favorite bite-size snacks and then bake. You're guaranteed a gift that will heat up the holidays!

JALAPEÑO SNACK MIX

- 1 package (16 ounces) cheese snack crackers
- 1 package (10 ounces) small pretzel twists
- 1 package (12 ounces) square corn cereal
- 1/2 cup drained pickled jalapeño pepper slices
- 2 tablespoons Dijon-style mustard
- 3 cloves garlic, coarsely chopped
- 1 teaspoon dried oregano leaves
- 2 teaspoons ground cumin
- 3/4 cup butter or margarine

Preheat oven to 250 degrees. Place crackers, pretzels, and cereal in a large roasting pan. Process jalapeño peppers, mustard, garlic, oregano, and cumin in a small food processor until peppers and garlic are finely chopped. In a medium microwave-safe bowl, combine pepper mixture and butter. Cover and microwave on medium power (50%) until butter melts. Pour over cereal mixture; toss until well coated. Bake 1¼ hours, stirring every 15 minutes. Spread on aluminum foil to cool. For each gift, place 1½ cups in a small cellophane bag; fold and staple top to secure.

Yield: about 22 cups snack mix

HOT PEPPER SLEEVES

For each sleeve, you will need white, yellow, red, and green card stock; decorative-edge craft scissors; tracing paper; 4½" x 14" piece of kraft paper; glue stick; black permanent fine-point marker; hole punch; and several 18" lengths of red and natural raffia.

1. Cut a 4¼" x 5" piece from yellow card stock; cut two ½" x 4¼" strips from green card stock. Using craft scissors, cut two ½" x 4" strips from white card stock.
2. Trace patterns, page 105, onto tracing paper; cut out. Using patterns, cut one highlight from white card stock, one stem from green card stock, and one pepper and two pointed strips from red card stock.
3. Arrange and glue shapes and strips on yellow card stock. Glue yellow card stock to kraft paper ½" from one short edge.
4. Use marker to write "Hot" and draw swirls and dots on yellow card stock.
5. To form sleeve, fold each end of kraft paper 5½" to wrong side. Punch two holes 1" apart at center top of sleeve. Thread raffia through holes and tie into a bow. Place gift in sleeve.

CHERRY DELIGHT

*S*erved warm over pound cake or ice cream, this Special Cherry Cobbler Topping is tops! Sweet, dark cherries in a thick, rich syrup will please the palate. Place a jar of the topping and a loaf of pound cake in a basket embellished with buttons and bows for a gift that's clad in country charm.

SPECIAL CHERRY COBBLER TOPPING

   1 can (16 ounces) pitted dark
        cherries in heavy syrup
   3 tablespoons sugar
   1 tablespoon cornstarch
   1 teaspoon freshly squeezed lemon
        juice
   2 tablespoons Chambord (raspberry-
        flavored liqueur)
        Pound cake to serve

Drain cherries, reserving ½ cup syrup. Process cherries in a food processor until coarsely chopped. In a small saucepan, combine cherries, sugar, cornstarch, lemon juice, and reserved cherry syrup. Stirring constantly, cook over medium-low heat until mixture comes to a boil. Continuing to stir, cook 1 minute or until mixture thickens. Remove from heat and stir in liqueur. Serve warm over pound cake or ice cream. Store in an airtight container in refrigerator.

Yield: about 1⅓ cups topping

BUTTON BASKET

You will need a round basket (we used a 6½" dia. basket with handle), fabric, string, fabric marking pen, thumbtack, polyester fiberfill, hot glue gun, assorted buttons, jute twine, decorative-edge craft scissors, card stock, craft glue, 3" x 4½" piece of corrugated craft cardboard, black permanent fine-point marker, hole punch, jar with lid, felt for jar lid cover, pinking shears, and a rubber band.

1. Measure basket from rim to rim (Fig. 1); add 4". Cut a square of fabric the determined measurement.

Fig. 1

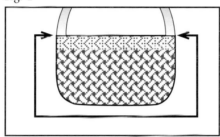

2. Matching right sides, fold fabric square in half from top to bottom, and again from left to right. Tie one end of string to fabric marking pen. Measure ½ the determined measurement in Step 1 from pen; insert thumbtack through string at this point. Insert thumbtack through fabric and keeping string taut, mark cutting line (Fig. 2). Cutting through all layers, cut out circle along drawn line.

Fig. 2

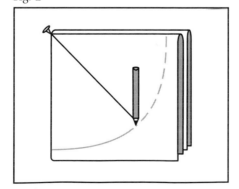

3. Work a *Running Stitch*, page 123, along edges of circle. Center basket on wrong side of circle. Pull ends of threads to begin gathering fabric under rim of basket. Lightly fill space between fabric and basket with fiberfill. Pull thread ends to tighten fabric around basket; knot ends together to secure. Adjust gathers as necessary. Hot glue gathers to basket and buttons around rim of basket. Tie a length of twine into a bow over gathers; knot ends.

4. For tag, use craft scissors to cut a 2½" x 3¾" piece from card stock. Using craft glue, glue card stock on cardboard; allow to dry. Matching short ends, fold tag in half. Tie a 9" length of twine into a bow. Hot glue bow and buttons to tag. Use marker to write message on tag. Punch hole in corner of tag. Use a 5" length of twine to attach tag to handle of basket.

5. Draw around jar lid on felt. Use pinking shears to cut out circle 1½" outside drawn line. Center felt circle over jar lid; secure with rubber band. Tie a length of twine into a bow around jar, covering rubber band.

GOLDEN TREASURES

A gold mine of flavor, our Orange-Walnut Bars are treasures to be savored! The golden nuggets get their start from orange cake mix and are finished with a rich, creamy topping. Trimmed with a plaid ribbon, a box topped with our special-delivery Santa makes a festive treasure chest.

ORANGE-WALNUT BARS

CRUST

  1 package (18 1/4 ounces) orange
      cake mix
 1/3 cup vegetable oil
 1/3 cup applesauce
  1 egg
  1 teaspoon vanilla extract
 2/3 cup flaked coconut

TOPPING

  1 cup sugar
 1/3 cup butter or margarine
 1/3 cup milk
  1 cup white baking chips
  1 cup chopped walnuts

Preheat oven to 350 degrees. Line a 9 x 13-inch baking pan with waxed paper; grease waxed paper. For crust, combine cake mix, oil, applesauce, egg, vanilla, and coconut in a medium bowl; beat until well blended. Spread mixture into prepared pan. Bake 20 to 25 minutes or until edges are lightly browned. While crust is baking, prepare topping.

For topping, combine sugar, butter, and milk in a heavy medium saucepan over medium-high heat. Stirring constantly, bring mixture to a boil and boil 1 minute. Reduce heat to low. Add baking chips; stir

until smooth. Stir in walnuts. Spread hot topping over warm crust. Cool in pan. Cut into 1 x 2-inch bars. Store in an airtight container.

Yield: about 4 dozen bars

SANTA CROSS STITCH BOX

You will need embroidery floss and blending filament (see color key, page 106), 10 1/2" square each of white Aida (14 ct) and paper-backed fusible web, 11" square papier-mâché box with lid, craft glue, four 1 1/2" x 11" strips of plaid fabric, and 17" of 1 1/2"w gold sheer wired ribbon.

Refer to Cross Stitch and Embroidery Stitches, page 123, before beginning project.

1. Using six strands of floss for *Cross Stitch,* two strands of floss for *Backstitch,* and four strands of floss for *French Knots,* stitch design, page 106, on Aida over two fabric threads.
2. Fuse web to wrong side of design. Center and fuse design on box lid.
3. Covering raw edges of stitched piece, glue fabric lengths along each edge. Tie gold ribbon into a bow; glue to lid at top of stitched oranament hanger.

ORNAMENTAL TREATS

*F*or a sweet surprise, hang our Round Ornament Cookies on a little tree. Made with ingredients you probably already have in the cupboard, the cookies are cut from a simple pattern and iced in bright colors. You'll want to have extra cookies for nibbling, too!

ROUND ORNAMENT COOKIES

COOKIES

- 1/2 cup butter or margarine, softened
- 1/3 cup vegetable shortening
- 1/2 cup granulated sugar
- 1/2 cup firmly packed brown sugar
- 1/4 cup dark corn syrup
- 1 egg
- 1 teaspoon vanilla extract
- 3 cups all-purpose flour
- 1/4 teaspoon salt

ICING

- 6 2/3 cups confectioners sugar
- 1/2 cup water
- 1 tablespoon light corn syrup
- 1 teaspoon vanilla extract
  Red, green, yellow, and blue paste food coloring

Trace ornament pattern, page 107, onto stencil plastic; cut out. Preheat oven to 350 degrees. For cookies, cream butter, shortening, and sugars in a large bowl until fluffy. Add corn syrup, egg, and vanilla; beat until smooth. In a medium bowl, combine flour and salt. Add dry ingredients to creamed mixture; stir until a soft dough forms. Divide dough in half. On a lightly floured surface, use a floured rolling pin to roll out half of dough to 1/8-inch thickness. Use pattern and a sharp knife to cut out cookies. Transfer to a greased baking sheet. Use a plastic drinking straw to cut a hole in top of each cookie. Bake 6 to 8 minutes or until bottoms are lightly browned. Transfer cookies to a wire rack to cool. Repeat with remaining dough.

For icing, combine confectioners sugar, water, corn syrup, and vanilla in a medium bowl; stir until smooth. Place 1/4 cup white icing in a small bowl and cover. Divide remaining icing into 4 small bowls; tint icing red, green, yellow, and blue. Spoon icing into pastry bags fitted with small round tips. Use tinted icing to pipe outline around edges of cookies; fill in with icing. Let icing harden. Use white icing to pipe highlight onto each cookie. Store in a single layer in an airtight container.

Yield: about 4 1/2 dozen cookies

FROSTY COOKIE BASKET

*S*hare the flavor of Christmas with a batch of snowflake-frosted Cinnamon Cookies. An ordinary basket becomes a wintry friend with the addition of a craft foam nose and colorful earmuffs made from juice can lids.

CINNAMON COOKIES

COOKIES

1¹/₂ cups vegetable shortening
3¹/₂ cups sugar
  2 eggs
¹/₂ cup water
  1 teaspoon vanilla extract
  5 cups all-purpose flour
  1 tablespoon ground cinnamon
  2 teaspoons baking powder
  1 teaspoon salt

ICING

³/₄ cup vegetable shortening
4¹/₄ cups confectioners sugar
  1 teaspoon vanilla extract
  4 to 5 tablespoons milk

Preheat oven to 375 degrees. For cookies, cream shortening and sugar in a large bowl until fluffy. Add eggs, water, and vanilla; beat until smooth. In a large bowl, combine flour, cinnamon, baking powder, and salt. Add dry ingredients to creamed mixture; stir until a soft dough forms. Shape dough into 1-inch balls and place 2 inches apart on a greased baking sheet; flatten balls into 2-inch-diameter cookies with bottom of a glass dipped in sugar. Bake 7 to 9 minutes or until bottoms are lightly browned. Transfer cookies to a wire rack to cool.

For icing, combine shortening, confectioners sugar, vanilla, and milk in a large bowl; beat until smooth. Spoon icing into a pastry bag fitted with a small star tip. Pipe snowflake design onto each cookie. Let icing harden. Store in an airtight container.

Yield: about 9 dozen cookies

SNOWMAN BASKET

You will need white spray paint, 7¹/₂" dia. basket, two lids from large frozen juice cans, red felt, red embroidery floss, hot glue gun, polyester fiberfill, orange and black craft foam, tracing paper, brown permanent medium-point marker, two black chenille stems, and two ⁵/₈" dia. black buttons for eyes.

1. Spray paint basket white; allow to dry.

2. For each earmuff, draw around lid on felt; cut out circle 1¹/₂" outside drawn line. Using floss, work *Running Stitches*, page 123, along edge of circle. Glue a small amount of fiberfill to one side of lid. Center lid fiberfill side down on felt circle. Pulling floss ends, gather felt over lid; knot ends together to secure.

3. For handle, cut a ³/₄" x 14" strip from black foam. Glue ends of strip to basket to form handle. Glue earmuffs over ends of handle.

4. Trace pattern, page 107, onto tracing paper; cut out. Using pattern, cut nose from orange foam. Use marker to draw detail lines on nose.

5. Shape one chenille stem into a wavy smile; position and glue on basket. Cut two 1¹/₂" pieces from remaining stem; glue one piece to each end of smile. Glue eyes and nose to basket.

POP-IN-THE-OVEN MUFFINS

A happy Noel is close at hand when you deliver the ingredients for our Christmas Cranberry Muffins along with instructions for making them. All the recipient has to do is add sour cream and bake! Tuck a bag of mix in an embroidered pot holder for a cheery presentation.

CHRISTMAS CRANBERRY MUFFINS

    2 cups all-purpose flour
    1 cup sugar
    1 teaspoon baking soda
    ½ teaspoon salt
    ½ cup chilled butter, cut into pieces
    1 cup sweetened dried cranberries, chopped
    ½ cup chopped pecans, toasted
    1½ teaspoons grated orange zest

In a medium bowl, combine flour, sugar, baking soda, and salt. Using pastry blender, cut butter into dry ingredients until mixture resembles coarse meal. Stir in cranberries, pecans, and orange zest. Divide mix into 2 resealable plastic bags. Store in refrigerator. Give with baking instructions.

Yield: 2 bags muffin mix, about 2½ cups each

To bake: In a medium bowl, combine 1 cup sour cream and 1 bag muffin mix (2½ cups); stir just until moistened. Fill paper-lined muffin cups full. Sprinkle with granulated sugar. Bake in a 400-degree oven 18 to 20 minutes or until a toothpick inserted in center of muffin comes out clean and tops are golden brown.

Yield: about 6 muffins

"NOEL" POT HOLDER

You will need tracing paper; pot holder with pocket; red, green, and brown embroidery floss; one ¾" dia. button; 6" x 22" piece of fabric; pinking shears; several 12" lengths of natural raffia; fabric for card; paper-backed fusible web; 3" x 5" piece of ecru card stock; and a black permanent fine-point marker.

Refer to Embroidery Stitches, page 123, before beginning project.

1. Trace pattern, page 107, onto tracing paper. Pin pattern to pot holder. Stitch design through paper using four strands of green floss to work *Stem Stitches* for holly, six strands of red floss to work *French Knots* for berries, and six strands of brown floss to work *Straight Stitches* for letters. Carefully tear away paper. Use floss to sew button in place for the "O" in NOEL.

2. For bag, matching right sides and short edges, fold fabric in half. Use a ¼" seam allowance to sew sides of bag. Turn bag right side out. Trim top of bag with pinking shears. Place gift in bag. Tie raffia into a bow around top of bag.

3. For card, cut one ½" x 5" strip each from fabric and web. Fuse web to fabric; fuse fabric along top edge of card stock. Use marker to write baking instructions on card.

4. Place bag and card in pocket of pot holder.

MERRY MINT MAYO

*S*pread holiday cheer with our Creamy Mint Mayonnaise! The flavorful combination of mayonnaise, mint leaves, and Dijon-style mustard will add zip to sandwiches or salads. A jar of this delightful dressing makes a festive gift when topped with a fabric circle that's tied with a buttoned-up bow.

CREAMY MINT MAYONNAISE

    2 cups mayonnaise
    2 cups packed mint leaves, finely
        chopped
    2 tablespoons Dijon-style mustard

In a small bowl, combine mayonnaise, mint, and mustard. Store in an airtight container in refrigerator. Use in place of plain mayonnaise on sandwiches and in salads.

Yield: about 2¼ cups mint mayonnaise

BUTTON AND BOWS JAR LID COVER

You will need a jar with lid, fabric, pinking shears, rubber band, two coordinating colors of ⅛"w ribbon, cotton string, hot glue gun, two buttons, spray adhesive, 1½" x 1¾" piece of ecru card stock, 2" x 2¼" piece of decorative paper, black permanent fine-point marker, and a hole punch.

1. Draw around jar lid on wrong side of fabric. Using pinking shears, cut out circle 2" outside drawn line.

2. Center fabric circle over jar lid; secure with rubber band. Measure around jar lid; add 8". Cut one length each from ribbons and string the determined measurement. Tie ribbons and string into a bow around lid, covering rubber band. Glue one button to knot of bow.

3. For tag, apply spray adhesive to one side of card stock; smooth onto decorative paper. Use marker to write message and draw "stitches" along edges of tag.

4. Punch hole in corner of tag. Use string to tie tag to gift. Glue remaining button to corner of tag.

34

PICKLES TO RELISH

A snap to make, our Sweet and Spicy Holiday Pickles are simply hamburger dills that you layer with sugar and marinate with vinegar and spices. Presented in a jar with a festive fabric topper, the crisp treats are gifts your friends and family will relish!

SWEET AND SPICY HOLIDAY PICKLES

- 1 jar (1 gallon) hamburger dill pickle slices, drained
- 6 cups sugar
- 1 cup apple cider vinegar
- 1 tablespoon pickling spice
- 2 teaspoons whole allspice
- 4 cinnamon sticks

In a gallon jar with lid, layer pickle slices and sugar in several layers. In a small microwave-safe bowl, combine vinegar, pickling spice, allspice, and cinnamon sticks. Microwave on high power (100%) until mixture boils. Pour hot mixture over pickles. Tightly screw on jar lid. Store pickles at room temperature 48 hours or until sugar dissolves, inverting jar twice a day and storing upright. Store in refrigerator. Serve chilled.

Yield: about 3 quarts pickles

JAR TOPPER

You will need a jar with lid, fabric, pinking shears, rubber band, jute twine, hot glue gun, artificial greenery (we used pine stems and berries), hole punch, and a gift tag.

1. Draw around jar lid on wrong side of fabric. Using pinking shears, cut out circle 2¹/₂" outside drawn line. Center fabric circle over lid and secure with rubber band.
2. Measure around lid; add 12". Cut two lengths of twine the determined length. Tie twine lengths into a bow around lid, covering rubber band.
3. Glue greenery under bow. Punch hole in corner of tag; thread tag onto twine streamer.

STIR IT UP!

If your gift list includes some folks who like to stir things up, surprise them with a batch of our spicy Stir-Fry Sauce. It's great in a variety of dishes, such as our Stir-Fry Chicken. Turn your gift into an authentic Oriental dinner by including the recipe, chow mein noodles, fortune cookies, green tea, and chopsticks.

STIR-FRY SAUCE

Include chow mein noodles, fortune cookies, green tea, and chopsticks with sauce.

- 1/4 cup soy sauce
- 1/4 cup oyster sauce (in Oriental section of supermarket)
- 2 tablespoons freshly squeezed lime juice
- 1 tablespoon freshly grated gingerroot
- 1 tablespoon sugar
- 1/2 teaspoon crushed red pepper flakes

In a small bowl, combine soy sauce, oyster sauce, lime juice, gingerroot, sugar, and red pepper flakes. Store in an airtight container in refrigerator. Give sauce with purchased items and recipe for Stir-Fry Chicken.

Yield: about 2/3 cup sauce

STIR-FRY CHICKEN

- Stir-Fry Sauce
- 1 pound skinless, boneless chicken breasts, cut into bite-size pieces
- 3 tablespoons dark sesame oil, divided
- 3 carrots, peeled and cut into thin diagonal slices
- 1 large green pepper, thinly sliced
- 1 large sweet red pepper, thinly sliced
- 1 large onion, thinly sliced
- 1 package (8 ounces) fresh mushrooms, sliced
- 4 cups cooked rice to serve

Pour Stir-Fry Sauce over chicken in a shallow dish. Cover and refrigerate 30 minutes, stirring after 15 minutes. Drain chicken, reserving sauce. In a large skillet or wok, heat 2 tablespoons sesame oil over medium-high heat. Stirring constantly, cook chicken 5 minutes or until chicken is tender. Remove chicken and set aside. Add remaining tablespoon sesame oil to skillet. Add carrots, peppers, and onion. Stir fry on medium high 5 minutes or until vegetables are crisp tender. Stir in chicken, mushrooms, and reserved sauce. Bring sauce to a boil; cook about 2 minutes or until mushrooms are tender. Serve warm over rice with chow mein noodles on top.

Yield: 6 to 8 servings

STIR-FRY SAUCE LABEL

You will need tracing paper, transfer paper, 1 1/2" square of white card stock, black permanent fine-point marker, craft glue, and a jar with lid.

1. Trace pattern, page 107, onto tracing paper. Use transfer paper to transfer pattern to center of card stock.
2. Use marker to trace over words.
3. Glue label to jar.

DINNER'S IN THE BAG!

*A*re your friends too busy during the holidays to enjoy a hot, home-cooked meal together? With this quick-to-fix treat, dinner's in the bag! Put a container of our spicy-sweet Sloppy Joe sauce in an appliquéd grocery bag, and don't forget to throw in the buns. Your friends will appreciate this homemade twist on take-out.

SLOPPY JOES

　　3　pounds ground beef
　1¹/₂　cups finely chopped onions
　　¹/₂　cup finely chopped green pepper
　　¹/₂　cup finely chopped sweet
　　　　red pepper
　　1　bottle (40 ounces) ketchup
　　1　tablespoon garlic powder
　1¹/₂　teaspoons salt
　　³/₄　teaspoon ground black pepper
　　　　Sandwich buns to serve

In a large skillet, brown ground beef over medium-high heat; drain. Reduce heat to medium. Add onions and green and red peppers to meat. Stirring frequently, cook until vegetables are tender. Stir in ketchup, garlic powder, salt, and black pepper. Reduce heat to medium low. Stirring frequently, cook uncovered 15 minutes. Serve warm over buns. Store in an airtight container in refrigerator.

Yield: about 8 cups sauce

DINNER IN A BAG

You will need a large brown paper grocery bag, fabrics for appliqués, paper-backed fusible web, pliers, hot glue gun, assorted buttons, two two-prong paper fasteners, two 1" dia. buttons with two holes, black permanent fine-point marker, sharp needle, and embroidery floss.

Refer to Making Appliqués, page 121, before beginning project.

1. Cut 4" from top of each side of bag; set paper pieces aside.
2. For background, measure width and height of front of bag; subtract ¹/₂" from each measurement. Make background appliqué using the determined measurements. Fuse appliqué to front of bag.
3. Using patterns, page 108, make two

trunk, three tree, and three background tree appliqués. Arrange and fuse appliqués on background. Hot glue assorted buttons to trees.
4. Place gift in bag. For each button closure, use pliers to bend each post on fastener in half lengthwise. Insert posts through button holes. Fold top flap over bottom flap. Push fastener through both flaps; spread fastener posts to secure.
5. For tag, cut a 3" square from remaining paper piece. Cut four ¹/₂" x 3" strips each from web and fabric. Fuse web strips to fabric strips; fuse fabric strips along edges of tag. Use marker to draw "stitches" and write message on tag. Using needle, thread a 6" length of floss through corner of tag; knot ends together. Loop floss around one button.

SPECIAL DELIVERY

F or a first-class gift, send a special delivery of our Orange-Maple Mustard. The quick-to-fix sauce makes an excellent glaze for chicken or pork and will add pizzazz to plain sandwiches. A "recycled" snack food can decorated with stamp motif wrapping paper makes sure your gift reaches its destination in holiday style.

ORANGE-MAPLE MUSTARD

- 1 jar (24 ounces) prepared mustard
- 2/3 cup orange marmalade
- 1/2 cup maple syrup
- 2 tablespoons minced onion

In a medium bowl, combine mustard, marmalade, maple syrup, and onion. Store in an airtight container in refrigerator.

Yield: about 4 cups mustard

SANTA STAMP CAN

You will need a jar with lid, kraft paper, decorative-edge craft scissors, rubber band, jute twine, stamp-motif and red wrapping paper, craft glue, black permanent fine-point marker, can large enough to accommodate jar, spray adhesive, hammer, nail, 14" of craft wire, and decorative tissue paper.

1. For jar topper, draw around jar lid on kraft paper. Using craft scissors, cut out circle 1 1/2" outside drawn line. Center circle over lid; secure with rubber band. Measure around lid; add 16". Cut a length of twine the determined measurement. Tie twine into a bow, covering rubber band.

2. For stamp, use craft scissors to cut a stamp motif from wrapping paper. Glue motif to jar topper; allow to dry. Use marker to draw wavy lines across stamp.
3. Measure height of can between rims. Measure around can; add 1/2". Cut a piece from red wrapping paper the determined measurements. Apply spray adhesive to wrong side of paper; smooth paper around can. Repeat to add a strip of stamp-motif paper around can.
4. For handle, use hammer and nail to punch a hole on each side of can. Insert one end of wire through one hole; curl end of wire to secure. Repeat for opposite hole.
5. Line can with tissue paper. Place jar in can.

39

SOUTHERN-STYLE BREAD

A Southern variation of pumpkin bread, our Sweet Potato Quick Bread is bursting with goodness. The moist, nutty snack starts with biscuit mix and quick-cooking oats and gets its crunch from chopped walnuts. A kitchen towel appliquéd with evergreens and fashioned into a bag makes a festive package for the spicy bread.

SWEET POTATO QUICK BREAD

BREAD
    2   cups all-purpose baking mix
    3/4 cup firmly packed brown sugar
    1/2 cup quick-cooking oats
    1 1/2 teaspoons ground cinnamon
    1/8 teaspoon ground cloves
    1/8 teaspoon ground nutmeg
    1   cup cooked, mashed sweet potatoes
    1/2 cup milk
    2   eggs
    1/4 cup butter or margarine, melted
    1/2 cup chopped walnuts

TOPPING
    2   tablespoons chopped walnuts
    2   tablespoons firmly packed brown sugar
    2   tablespoons quick-cooking oats
    2   tablespoons butter, melted

Preheat oven to 350 degrees. For bread, combine baking mix, brown sugar, oats, cinnamon, cloves, and nutmeg in a large bowl. In a medium bowl, combine sweet potatoes, milk, eggs, and melted butter; beat until well blended. Stir into dry ingredients; beat until blended. Stir in walnuts. Spoon into a greased 5 x 9-inch loaf pan.

For topping, combine walnuts, brown sugar, oats, and melted butter in a small bowl; stir until blended. Sprinkle topping over batter. Bake 45 to 55 minutes or until a toothpick inserted in center of bread comes out with a few crumbs attached. Cool in pan 5 minutes. Remove from pan and cool completely on a wire rack. Store in an airtight container.

Yield: 1 loaf bread

APPLIQUÉD TOWEL BAG

You will need a kitchen towel 17"w and at least 19" long, 3/4"w paper-backed fusible web tape, paper-backed fusible web, fabric, natural raffia, hot glue gun, two 3/4" dia. buttons, and 27" of 5/8"w grosgrain ribbon.

1. If necessary, trim length of towel to measure 19".
2. Press fusible tape along one short, then one long edge on right side of towel; do not overlap tape ends. Remove paper backing from short edge. Matching right sides and short edges, fold towel in half; fuse in place. Remove paper backing from long edge. Fold tube with seam at center back (Fig. 1); fuse in place. Turn bag right side out.

Fig. 1

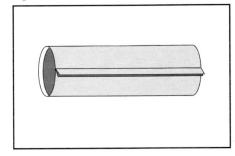

3. Using pattern, page 109, follow *Making Appliqués*, page 121, to make two tree appliqués from fabric. Fuse trees to front of bag.
4. For each tree, tie an 11" length of raffia into a bow. Glue bow to top of tree and button to knot of bow.
5. Place gift in bag. Tie ribbon into a bow around top of bag.

ELVES' ENERGY BOOSTERS

*T*he hustle and bustle of the holidays can tire even the most dedicated of Santa's helpers. Why not provide them with an energy booster that tastes great! For a gift that will look like it came straight from the North Pole, wrap our granola bars in gold foil and attach nifty photocopied labels.

NORTH POLE GRANOLA BARS

- $^1/_4$ cup butter or margarine, softened
- $^3/_4$ cup firmly packed brown sugar
- $^1/_2$ cup crunchy peanut butter
- $^1/_4$ cup light corn syrup
- 1 egg
- 1 teaspoon vanilla extract
- $^3/_4$ cup all-purpose flour
- $^1/_2$ teaspoon baking powder
- $1^1/_2$ cups quick-cooking oats
- 2 packages (6 ounces each) chopped dried fruit
- $^1/_2$ cup chopped salted peanuts

Preheat oven to 325 degrees. Line a 9 x 13-inch baking pan with aluminum foil, extending foil over ends of pan. Lightly grease foil. In a medium bowl, cream butter and brown sugar until fluffy. Add peanut butter, corn syrup, egg, and vanilla; beat until smooth. In a small bowl, combine flour and baking powder. Add dry ingredients to creamed mixture; stir until a soft dough forms. Stir in oats, fruit, and peanuts. Press mixture into prepared pan. Bake 30 to 33 minutes or until firm and lightly browned. Cool in pan. Use ends of foil to lift from pan. Cut into 2 x 4-inch bars. Wrap individually or store in an airtight container.

Yield: about 1 dozen bars

42

GRANOLA WRAPPERS

For each bar, you will need colored pencils, a photocopy of wrapper design (page 105) on white paper, 6" x 6½" piece of gold foil, and craft glue.

1. Use colored pencils to color wrapper design; cut out wrapper.

2. Center bar on wrong side of foil; wrap bar gift-wrap style.

3. Overlapping ends at back, wrap wrapper around bar. Glue overlapped ends to secure.

HAPPY FACE SURPRISES

A child's school Christmas party will be even more fun with these happy-face party cups filled with Old-fashioned Caramel Corn. The sweet treats are guaranteed to produce smiles on children and adults. Don't forget to hide a prize in each cup for an added surprise!

OLD-FASHIONED CARAMEL CORN

16 cups popped popcorn
 2 cups firmly packed brown sugar
 1/2 cup molasses
 1/2 cup butter or margarine
 1 teaspoon salt
 1 teaspoon vanilla extract
 1 teaspoon baking soda

Preheat oven to 250 degrees. Place popcorn in a greased large roasting pan. In a large saucepan, combine brown sugar, molasses, butter, and salt over medium heat. Stirring constantly, bring to a boil; boil 1 minute. Remove from heat. Stir in vanilla and baking soda (mixture will foam). Pour over popcorn; stir until well coated. Bake 30 minutes, stirring after 15 minutes. Spread on greased aluminum foil to cool. Store in an airtight container.

Yield: about 17 cups caramel corn

SURPRISE PARTY CUPS

For each cup, you will need a small toy for prize, 8-oz. party cup, 4" x 7" clear cellophane bag, one 24" length each of white and green curling ribbon, white paper, hole punch, and a black permanent fine-point marker.

1. Place prize in bottom of cup. Fill cup with popcorn and place in cellophane bag. Tie ribbons into a bow around top of bag. Curl ribbon ends.

2. For tag, cut a triangle-shaped tag from paper. Punch hole in top corner. Use marker to write message on tag. Thread one curled ribbon through hole to secure.

COOKIE CUPS

For a treat that's as easy to fix as it is good to eat, try these Chocolate-Peanut Butter Cups. Using a package of refrigerated peanut butter cookie dough makes quick work of gift-giving. Jazz up a plain white box with painted stars and swirls and tie with ribbon for a sparkling presentation.

CHOCOLATE-PEANUT BUTTER CUPS

  1 package (18 ounces) refrigerated peanut butter cookie dough
  1 bag (13 ounces) mini peanut butter cups

Preheat oven to 350 degrees. Shape dough into 1-inch balls. Place balls in greased cups of a miniature muffin pan. Press peanut butter cups into center of each ball. Bake 10 to 12 minutes or until edges are firm. Cool in pan 5 minutes. Remove from pan and cool completely on a wire rack. Store in an airtight container.

Yield: about 3 dozen cookies

GREEN STAR CANDY BOX

You will need a 6³/8" x 9³/8" x 1¹/4" gift box; white wrapping paper; tape; tracing paper; compressed craft sponge; gold, red, and green acrylic paint; paintbrush; old toothbrush; paper towels; 1²/3 yds. of ³/8"w gold mesh wired ribbon; 26" of ¹/2"w red wired ribbon; 17" of 1¹/2"w green sheer ribbon; 6" of gold cord; and a purchased gift tag.

Refer to Sponge Painting and Spatter Painting, page 122, before beginning project.

1. Wrap box lid gift-wrap style with white paper. Trace pattern, page 109, onto tracing paper; cut out. Using pattern, cut star shape from sponge. Sponge paint green stars on lid. Paint red swirls on lid. Spatter paint lid gold; allow to dry.
2. Place gift in box. Beginning with center of gold ribbon across top of box, wrap ribbon to bottom, twist ribbon at bottom, and bring ends to top of box; knot at center.
3. Using red ribbon, follow *Making a Bow*, page 121, to make a bow with four 6" loops and two 3" streamers. Use green ribbon to make a second bow with two 5" loops and two 3" streamers. Position red and green bows over knot of gold ribbon. Tie gold ribbon ends into a bow around red and green bows.
4. Use cord to attach tag to bow.

ESPRESSO ELEGANCE

*Y*ou can "espress" your sentiments to that special someone with our Cappuccino Nut Crunch. For an elegant presentation, wrap the treats in cellophane and place in a beribboned cone made from a dinner napkin.

CAPPUCCINO NUT CRUNCH

- 2 tablespoons hot water
- 1/2 teaspoon espresso powder
- 1 3/4 cups whole almonds, toasted
- 3/4 cup flaked coconut
- 1 cup plus 2 tablespoons sugar
- 1/3 cup whipping cream
- 1/4 cup butter
- 2 teaspoons light corn syrup
- 1/2 teaspoon ground cinnamon
- 1/2 teaspoon salt

In a small bowl, combine water and espresso powder; set aside. In another small bowl, combine almonds and coconut. Spread in a single layer in a greased 10 1/2 x 15 1/2-inch jellyroll pan. Butter sides of a heavy medium saucepan. Combine sugar, whipping cream, butter, corn syrup, cinnamon, salt, and espresso mixture in saucepan. Stirring constantly, cook over medium-low heat until sugar dissolves. Using a pastry brush dipped in hot water, wash down any sugar crystals on sides of pan. Attach a candy thermometer to pan, making sure thermometer does not touch bottom of pan. Increase heat to medium and bring to a boil. Cook, without stirring, until mixture reaches 290 degrees. Test about 1/2 teaspoon mixture in ice

water. Mixture will form hard threads in ice water but will soften when removed from water. Pour mixture in a thin stream over nut mixture; do not stir. Let cool; break into pieces. Store in an airtight container.

Yield: about 1 1/2 pounds candy

NAPKIN GIFT CONE

You will need 18" each of 2 1/4"w wired ribbon and gold cord, 20" square fabric napkin, 1 1/4" dia. button, 5" x 12" clear cellophane bag, 3 1/4" x 4" piece of card stock, and gold and silver permanent fine-point markers.

1. Tie ribbon into a bow.
2. Matching wrong sides, fold napkin in half from top to bottom and again from left to right.
3. With finished edges of napkin at top and overlapping edges at front, shape napkin into a cone. Centering button on bow, sew button and bow to front of cone to secure shape.
4. Place cellophane bag in cone. Place gift in bag. Tie cord into a bow around top of bag.
5. For tag, match short ends and fold card stock in half. Use gold marker to write message and draw leaves and berries on tag. Use silver marker to add details to leaves.

45

NATURAL WONDERS

*I*f you're looking for a gift that's as naturally appealing as it is delicious, then you'll want to try these Banana-Nut Cookies. Brown and green gift bags, stamped with various leaves and tied with coordinating ribbon, complement the offering. Because the cookies freeze well, you can keep several batches on hand for last-minute gifts.

BANANA-NUT COOKIES

These cookies freeze well.

- 2 packages (7.6 ounces each) banana-nut muffin mix
- 1 cup quick-cooking oats
- 1/4 teaspoon ground cinnamon
- 2 eggs
- 1/4 cup vegetable oil
- 2 tablespoons milk

Preheat oven to 350 degrees. In a medium bowl, combine muffin mix, oats, and cinnamon. In a small bowl, beat eggs, oil, and milk until blended. Add to dry ingredients; stir until a soft dough forms. Drop tablespoonfuls of dough onto an ungreased baking sheet. Bake 10 to 12 minutes or until bottoms are lightly browned. Transfer cookies to a wire rack to cool. Store in an airtight container.

Yield: about 3 dozen cookies

LEAF PRINT PAPER BAGS

For each bag, you will need gold or green acrylic paint, fresh or artificial greenery, paper gift bag with handles, tissue paper, assorted ribbons, and gold cord.

1. Using gold or green paint and greenery in place of a sponge shape, follow *Sponge Painting,* page 122, to paint leaf shapes on bag; allow to dry.

2. Line bag with tissue paper; place gift in bag.

3. Tie several lengths of ribbon and cord into a bow around handles of bag.

O CHRISTMAS TREE

O Christmas tree, O Christmas tree, how tasty are your branches! This Pistachio Fudge is holiday "greenery" at its best. Deliver your gift in a tree-shaped papier-mâché box that has been painted green, decorated with swirl ornaments, and topped with a wooden star.

PISTACHIO FUDGE

1¹/₂ cups sugar
  1 package (3.4 ounces) pistachio instant pudding mix
²/₃ cup evaporated milk
  2 tablespoons butter or margarine
¹/₄ teaspoon salt
  2 cups miniature marshmallows
1¹/₂ cups white baking chips
  1 teaspoon vanilla extract
¹/₂ cup chopped pistachios, divided

Line a 9-inch square baking pan with aluminum foil, extending foil over 2 sides of pan; grease foil. In a heavy large saucepan, combine sugar, pudding mix, evaporated milk, butter, and salt. Stirring constantly, bring mixture to a boil over medium heat; boil 5 minutes. Remove from heat. Stir in marshmallows, baking chips, and vanilla until smooth. Reserving 2 tablespoons pistachios, stir in remaining nuts. Spread mixture into prepared pan. Sprinkle reserved nuts on top. Chill 2 hours or until firm.

Use ends of foil to lift fudge from pan. Cut into 1-inch squares. Store in an airtight container.

Yield: about 5 dozen pieces fudge

PAINTED TREE BOX

You will need a papier-mâché box with lid (we used a 6" x 6" tree-shaped box with a cellophane window in lid); gold, green, and dark green acrylic paint; paintbrushes; household sponge; gold fine-point paint pen; 2"w wooden star; black permanent fine-point marker; and a hot glue gun.

1. Paint lid dark green. Follow *Sponge Painting*, page 122, to lightly paint top of lid green. Allow paint to dry after each application.
2. Use gold pen to paint swirls and dots on top of lid.
3. Using acrylic paint, paint wooden star gold. Use marker to write message on star; glue star to lid.

to: Rose

Spice
Coffee
Cake

2 cups all-purpose flour
1 cup firmly packed brown sugar
1¼ teaspoons baking spice, divided
½ cup chilled butter or margarine
1 cup buttermilk
1 teaspoon baking soda
1 egg
1 teaspoon vanilla extract
½ cup chopped walnuts

(over—→)

Add a little spice to someone's holidays with this aromatic offering! Memories of Grandma's kitchen will come to mind as the sweet savor of our baking spice wafts through the air. For a gift with homemade appeal, fill a decorative recipe box with a bag of seasonings and a set of handmade recipe cards. Be sure to include a few recipes of such favorites as our Spice Coffee Cake. Bows of raffia and torn fabric strips dress up your gift basket.

BAKING SPICE

 6 tablespoons ground cinnamon
 1 tablespoon ground allspice
 2 teaspoons ground nutmeg
 1 teaspoon ground cloves
 1/2 teaspoon ground ginger

In a medium bowl, combine cinnamon, allspice, nutmeg, cloves, and ginger. Substitute baking spice in cake, muffin, or bread recipes that use any of the above spices. Can also be sprinkled on hot cereal or toast. Give with recipe for Spice Coffee Cake.

Yield: about 1/2 cup baking spice

SPICE COFFEE CAKE

 2 cups all-purpose flour
 1 cup firmly packed brown sugar
 11/4 teaspoons Baking Spice, divided
 1/2 cup chilled butter or margarine, cut into pieces
 1 cup buttermilk
 1 teaspoon baking soda
 1 egg
 1 teaspoon vanilla extract
 1/2 cup chopped walnuts

Preheat oven to 350 degrees. In a large bowl, combine flour, brown sugar, and 1 teaspoon baking spice. Using a pastry blender or 2 knives, cut in butter until mixture resembles coarse meal. Reserve 1/2 cup of crumb mixture. In a small bowl, combine buttermilk and baking soda. Add buttermilk mixture, egg, and vanilla to remaining crumb mixture; stir just until moistened. Pour batter into a greased 9-inch square baking pan. Combine reserved crumb mixture, walnuts, and remaining 1/4 teaspoon baking spice. Sprinkle over batter.

Bake 27 to 30 minutes or until a toothpick inserted in center of cake comes out clean. Cool cake in pan 15 minutes. Cut into 2-inch squares and serve warm.

Yield: about 16 servings

DECORATED RECIPE BOXES AND CARDS

For each gift, you will need a basket (we used a 53/4" x 71/2" basket), fabric, natural excelsior, paper-backed fusible web, 3" x 5" cards cut from card stock, black permanent fine-point marker, raffia, decorative recipe box to hold 3" x 5" cards, decorative-edge craft scissors, kraft paper, hole punch, and 8" of 1/4"w ribbon.

Refer to Making Appliqués, page 121, before beginning project.

1. Measure around rim of basket; add 9". Tear a 11/4"w strip from fabric the determined length. Tie fabric into a bow around basket. Line basket with excelsior.
2. For each recipe card, make two 1/4" x 5" appliqués from fabric; fuse to card. Use marker to draw "stitches" around edges of cards and write recipe on card. Tie raffia into a bow around a stack of cards or place cards inside box. Tie several strands of raffia into a bow around recipe box.
3. For tag, use craft scissors to cut a 2" x 3" piece from kraft paper. Make two 3/8" x 11/2" appliqués and two 3/8" x 25/8" appliqués from fabric. Fuse short, then long appliqués on tag. Use marker to write message on tag. Punch hole in corner of tag. Use ribbon to tie tag to raffia on recipe box.

PEPPERED PEACH BUTTER

*T*he sweetness of peaches and the spiciness of jalapeño peppers harmonize in this flavorful spread. Colorful Jalapeño Peach Butter is given rustic appeal by topping a jar with checked fabric tied with a jute bow and placing it in a hanging basket.

JALAPEÑO PEACH BUTTER

3 cans (15 ounces each) sliced peaches packed in juice, drained
1/4 cup seeded and chopped red jalapeño peppers
2 cups sugar
1/4 teaspoon ground allspice

Process peaches and jalapeño peppers in a food processor until finely chopped. Combine peach mixture, sugar, and allspice in a 4¹/₂-quart Dutch oven. Stirring constantly, bring to a boil over medium-high heat. Reduce heat to medium low. Stirring frequently, cook mixture 20 minutes or until thickened. Spoon mixture into heat-resistant jars; cover and cool to room temperature. Store in refrigerator. Serve with cream cheese and crackers.

Yield: about 4¹/₄ cups peach butter

JAR LID TOPPER AND TAG

You will need a jar to fit in basket, fabric, jute twine, hanging basket (we used a 3¹/₂" dia. x 7¹/₂"h basket), tracing paper, ecru card stock, black permanent fine-point marker, and a hot glue gun.

1. For jar lid topper, measure across widest part of jar lid; add 3¹/₂". Tear a square from fabric the determined measurement. Center fabric square on jar lid. Tie twine into a bow around lid. Place jar in basket.

2. For tag, trace pattern, page 109, onto tracing paper; cut out. Using pattern, cut tag from card stock. Use marker to draw dots along edges and write message on tag. Glue tag to basket.

SANTA'S SPICY SPREAD

This Spicy Bean and Tomato Spread has just the right zip to make the taste buds tingle! For a jolly presentation, place a jar of spread and a bag of baguette slices in a Christmas container and tie with a bright bow.

SPICY BEAN AND TOMATO SPREAD

This spread is for garlic lovers!

- 1 cup boiling water
- 1/2 cup finely chopped sun-dried tomatoes
- 2 cans (15.8 ounces each) great Northern beans
- 3 cloves garlic, chopped
- 2 tablespoons olive oil
- 1 tablespoon freshly squeezed lemon juice
- 1/2 teaspoon ground cumin
- 1/2 teaspoon ground coriander
- 1/2 teaspoon salt
- 1/8 teaspoon ground red pepper
- 1/4 cup finely chopped fresh cilantro
  Baguette slices to serve

In a small heatproof bowl, pour boiling water over tomatoes. Cover and let stand 20 minutes; drain.

Rinse and drain beans. Process beans, garlic, oil, lemon juice, cumin, coriander, salt, and red pepper in a large food processor until smooth. Transfer to a medium bowl; stir in drained tomatoes and cilantro. Cover and chill at least 2 hours to let flavors blend. Serve spread at room temperature on toasted baguette slices.

Yield: about 2 1/2 cups spread

HOBBY NUTS

The hobby enthusiasts on your list will go nuts over these perky gift bags! Filled with plenty of Chocolate-Nut Popcorn for snacking while enjoying favorite pastimes, the plaid packages feature peanut characters portraying various leisure activities.

CHOCOLATE-NUT POPCORN

- 16 cups popped popcorn
- 1 can (11½ ounces) mixed nuts
- 1¼ cups sugar
- ¾ cup light corn syrup
- ¼ cup butter or margarine
- ½ teaspoon salt
- 1 package (6 ounces) semisweet chocolate chips
- 1 teaspoon chocolate extract
- 1 teaspoon vanilla extract

Preheat oven to 250 degrees. Place popcorn in a greased large roasting pan. In a heavy medium saucepan, combine nuts, sugar, corn syrup, butter, and salt over medium-high heat. Stirring constantly, bring to a boil; remove from heat. Add chocolate chips and extracts; stir until chocolate melts. Pour chocolate mixture over popcorn; stir until well coated. Bake popcorn 1 hour, stirring every 15 minutes. Spread on waxed paper and allow to cool. Break into pieces. Store in an airtight container in a cool place.

Yield: about 19 cups popcorn

HOBBY NUT GIFT BAGS

GIFT BAG

You will need red and green card stock, decorative-edge craft scissors, low-temperature glue gun, hole punch, black permanent fine-point marker, 5" x 10" cellophane bag, twist tie, 24" of jute twine, and a lunch-size gift bag.

1. For tag, cut a 2¹⁄₂" x 2⁷⁄₈" piece from red card stock. Use craft scissors to cut a 2¹⁄₄" x 2¹⁄₂" piece from green card stock. Center and glue green card stock on red card stock. Punch hole in corner of tag. Use black marker to write message on tag.
2. Fill cellophane bag with snack mix and close with twist tie. Thread twine through hole in tag. Tie twine into a bow over twist tie. Place cellophane bag in gift bag.

BASIC CHARACTER

You will need tracing paper, tan craft foam, black permanent fine-point marker, and a low-temperature glue gun.

1. Trace basic character pattern, page 110, onto tracing paper; cut out. Using pattern, cut character from foam.
2. Use marker to draw swirl eyes and mouth on face and straight or cross "stitches" along edges of character.
3. Complete basic character with desired hobby-nut activity motifs; glue to front of gift bag.

GARDENING NUT

You will need a basic character; tracing paper; light green craft foam; craft knife; cutting mat; black permanent fine-point marker; low-temperature glue gun; and miniature artificial flowers, flowerpot, and gardening tool.

1. Trace gardening hat and apron patterns, page 110, onto tracing paper; cut out. Using patterns, cut hat and apron from foam. Use craft knife to make cut in hat as indicated on pattern.
2. Use marker to draw details on hat and apron.
3. Glue hat to head and flowers to hat. Glue apron to character. Glue arms around flowerpot and gardening tool.

COOKING NUT

You will need a basic character, tracing paper, white craft foam, decorative-edge craft scissors, black permanent fine-point marker, low-temperature glue gun, and a miniature cookbook and spoon.

1 Trace chef hat and apron patterns, page 110, onto tracing paper; cut out. Using patterns, cut hat and apron from foam. Use craft scissors to trim bottom edge of apron.
2. Use marker to draw details on hat and apron.
3. Glue hat and apron to character. Glue arms around cookbook and spoon.

GOLF NUT

You will need a basic character, tracing paper, green craft foam, black permanent fine-point marker, red dimensional paint, low-temperature glue gun, 7mm red pom-pom, and a miniature golf club.

1. Trace golf hat and pants patterns, page 110, onto tracing paper; cut out. Using patterns, cut hat and pants from foam.
2. Use marker, then paint to add detail lines to hat and pants; allow to dry.
3. Glue pom-pom to hat, hat and pants to character, and arms to club.

QUILTING NUT

You will need a basic character, needle-nose pliers, 3" of gold craft wire, two ¹⁄₂" long straight pins, a low-temperature glue gun, one 4" square each of fabric and lightweight fusible interfacing, pinking shears, #22 tapestry needle, and 8" of metallic thread.

1. Use pliers to shape wire into eyeglasses. Insert ends of glasses through face. Insert pins through corner of mouth. Glue wire ends and pins on back of character to secure.
2. For quilt, fuse interfacing to wrong side of fabric. Using pinking shears, trim edges of fabric. Fold fabric into quarters; glue right arm to fold of quilt. Thread needle with metallic thread. Glue left hand around needle and ends of thread behind quilt.

COMPUTER NUT

You will need a basic character, needle-nose pliers, 6" of black craft wire, low-temperature glue gun, and two miniature computer books.

1. Use pliers to shape wire into eyeglasses. Fold ends of wire over edges of face. Glue wire ends to back of character to secure.
2. Glue one arm around each book.

CHEERY CHERRY SANTA

Let our merry gift-giver deliver a taste of Yuletide cheer to your Christmas party with Cherry Lemonade! A gallon-size jar quickly transforms into a jolly face with dabs of white paint and some craft foam cutouts. Topped with a ready-made hat, Santa comes to life!

CHERRY LEMONADE

  1   can (16 ounces) frozen lemonade concentrate, thawed
1¹/₂ cups sugar
  1   package (0.13 ounce) unsweetened cherry-flavored soft drink mix
2¹/₂ quarts water
  1   jar (10 ounces) maraschino cherries

In a 1-gallon container, combine lemonade concentrate, sugar, and soft drink mix. Gradually add water, whisking until well blended. Add undrained cherries. Cover and chill.

Yield: about 13 cups lemonade

SANTA JAR WITH HAT

You will need tracing paper, tape, gallon-size jar with lid, compressed craft sponge, white Air-Dry Perm Enamel™ paint, white and brown craft foam, black permanent medium-point marker, hot glue gun, paintbrush, and a Santa hat.

Allow paint to dry after each application.

1. Trace patterns, page 111, onto tracing paper; cut out. Position and tape beard

pattern inside jar. Using pattern, cut circle from sponge. Following *Sponge Painting*, page 122, use white paint to sponge paint beard on outside of jar. Remove pattern from jar.
2. Using patterns, cut two eyebrows, two eyes, and mustache from white craft foam and two irises from brown craft foam. Use marker to draw a circle on each iris for pupil. Glue shapes to jar.
3. Use white paint and tip of paintbrush handle to add highlight to each eye.
4. Fill jar with lemonade; place lid on jar. Place hat on Santa.

LET IT SNOW!

Let it snow! On a cold, blustery day, your friends can stay inside and enjoy smooth Peppermint Cream Liqueur. The spirited beverage mixes up quickly with schnapps and vodka. Our appliquéd tote will remind folks to serve the creamy drink chilled.

PEPPERMINT CREAM LIQUEUR

1 1/2 cups whipping cream
  1 can (14 ounces) sweetened
     condensed milk
 1/2 cup peppermint schnapps
 1/4 cup vodka
  1 teaspoon vanilla extract

In a large bowl, combine whipping cream, sweetened condensed milk, peppermint schnapps, vodka, and vanilla. Beat at low speed of an electric mixer until blended. Pour into gift bottles. Store in refrigerator. Serve chilled.

Yield: about 3 3/4 cups liqueur

SNOWMAN CANVAS BAG

You will need white, orange, red, and black felt; paper-backed fusible web; two coordinating fabrics; pinking shears; canvas bag (we used a 7 1/2" x 13" canvas bag with handles); hot glue gun; four 1/2" dia. wooden buttons; one 1/4" dia. black pom-pom; five 3/8" dia. white buttons; two 5mm black cabochons for eyes; 1" of black embroidery floss for mouth; two 3/8" dia. green buttons; black permanent fine-point marker; and green raffia.

1. Using patterns, page 112, follow *Making Appliqués*, page 121, to make snowman from white felt, nose from orange felt, brim from red felt, and hat from black felt. Make one 5 1/4" x 7" background and one 6" x 8" border appliqué from coordinating fabrics. Trim border edges with pinking shears.
2. Fuse border to bag; fuse background to border. Arrange and fuse snowman appliqués on background. Glue wooden buttons to corners of background.

3. For scarf, cut one 1/4" x 7" strip from fabric. Cut a 2" piece from strip. Trimming to fit, glue 2" piece to neck. Tie a knot in center of remaining piece; glue knot to scarf.
4. Glue pom-pom to hat, white buttons along brim, eyes and mouth to face, and green buttons to front of snowman.
5. Use marker to write "Let it Snow!" across top of bag. Tie several lengths of raffia together into a bow; glue to bag.

A Christmas tradition in the making, our Chili Peanut Brittle is a unique gathering of sweet and savory flavors. Traditional sugar-and-corn syrup brittle meets a blend of peppers in this spiced-up creation. A beribboned jar of candy, tied with our polar pal cross stitch ornament, results in a gift that's twice as nice.

CHILI PEANUT BRITTLE

1	teaspoon paprika
1	teaspoon chili powder
1/2	teaspoon salt
1/8	teaspoon ground red pepper
1/8	teaspoon ground coriander
2	cups sugar
3/4	cup light corn syrup
1/4	cup water
1	package (12 ounces) raw Spanish peanuts
1/4	cup butter
1 1/2	teaspoons baking soda

In a small bowl, combine paprika, chili powder, salt, red pepper, and coriander; set aside.

Butter sides of a heavy large saucepan. Combine sugar, corn syrup, and water in saucepan. Stirring constantly, cook over medium-low heat until sugar dissolves. Using a pastry brush dipped in hot water, wash down any sugar crystals on sides of pan. Attach a candy thermometer to pan, making sure thermometer does not touch bottom of pan. Increase heat to medium and bring to a boil. Cook, without stirring, about 10 minutes or until mixture reaches 260 degrees. Stir in peanuts and continue cooking until mixture reaches hard-crack stage (approximately 300 to 310 degrees). Test about 1/2 teaspoon syrup in ice water. Mixture will form brittle threads in ice water and will remain brittle when removed from water. Remove from heat. Add butter and spice mixture; stir until butter melts. Add baking soda (syrup will foam); stir until soda dissolves. Pour candy onto a large piece of buttered aluminum foil; cool completely. Break into pieces. Store in an airtight container.

Yield: about 2 pounds candy

JAR WITH CROSS STITCH ORNAMENT

You will need embroidery floss and three red petite glass beads (see color key, page 113), 5" square of white Aida (18 ct), 2 1/2" dia. frame, jar with domed lid, 2 1/2"w wired ribbon, 5" of 1/8"w satin ribbon, white and green card stock, craft glue, decorative-edge craft scissors, and a black permanent fine-point marker.

Refer to Cross Stitch, page 123, before beginning project.

1. Using two strands of floss for *Cross Stitch* and one strand of floss for *Backstitch*, center and stitch design, page 113, on Aida.
2. Center and mount stitched design in frame.
3. Measure around jar lid; add 17". Cut a length of wired ribbon the determined measurement; tie into a bow around jar lid. Use satin ribbon to attach ornament to knot of bow.
4. For tag, cut a 1 5/8" x 2 1/4" piece from white card stock. Glue tag to green card stock. Leaving a 1/8" green border, use craft scissors to cut out tag. Use marker to write message on tag; glue tag to jar.

LIVELY LIMES

*E*nliven someone's Christmas breakfast with a jar of Lime Marmalade. Its zesty fruit flavor will taste great on fresh-from-the-oven biscuits or muffins. It's also a peppy appetizer when served with cream cheese and crackers. Your gift will take shape quickly when you place a jar of marmalade in a lined basket accented with greenery.

LIME MARMALADE

- ½ cup lime zest
- 3 cups lime juice (about 12 limes)
- 2½ cups water
- 1 package (1¾ ounces) powdered fruit pectin
- 8 cups sugar
  Green liquid food coloring

In a Dutch oven, combine zest, lime juice, water, and pectin over medium-high heat. Bring to a rolling boil. Add sugar. Stirring constantly, bring to a rolling boil again and boil 1 minute. Remove from heat; skim off foam. Tint green. Spoon marmalade into heat-resistant jars; cover and cool to room temperature. Store in refrigerator.

Yield: about 10½ cups marmalade

MARMALADE BASKET

You will need gold spray paint, small pinecone, hot glue gun, artificial greenery pick (we used holly leaves with berries), ¾" x 12" strip of green Mylar™ twist (untwisted), basket (we used an oval 5"h metallic red plastic basket), and green shredded Mylar™.

1. Paint pinecone gold; allow to dry. Glue pinecone to greenery.
2. Tie Mylar strip into a bow; glue to basket.
3. Line basket with shredded Mylar; place jar and greenery in basket.

CRANBERRY-ORANGE VINEGAR

Embellished with a jingle bell and a perky plaid bow, a clear decanter makes a striking showcase for our Cranberry-Orange Vinegar. The colorful condiment, made with fresh cranberries and orange juice, is a tasty topping for salads. It's also a great substitute for regular vinegar in your favorite recipes.

CRANBERRY-ORANGE VINEGAR

- 1 quart white vinegar
- 1 cup fresh cranberries
- ¹/₂ cup honey
- ¹/₄ cup freshly squeezed orange juice
- 2 teaspoons grated orange zest
  Fresh rosemary sprigs, washed, dried, and divided

Combine vinegar, cranberries, honey, orange juice, orange zest, and 1 sprig rosemary in a large non-aluminum saucepan. Bring mixture to a boil. Remove from heat and pour into a heatproof container. Cover and store in refrigerator overnight.

Strain mixture through cheesecloth into decorative containers. Place rosemary sprig in each container. Cover and store in refrigerator up to 2 weeks.

Yield: about 5 cups vinegar

CRUET WITH BOW

You will need 42" of ⁷/₈"w wired ribbon, 12" of floral wire, cruet (we used a 6¹/₂" tall cruet with handle and cork stopper), hot glue gun, ⁵/₈" dia. jingle bell, glue stick, green card stock, Christmas message cut from wrapping paper or card, black permanent fine-point markers, hole punch, and 6" of curling ribbon.

1. Use wired ribbon and follow *Making a Bow,* page 121, to make a bow with six 5" loops and two 4¹/₂" streamers. Use wire to attach bow to cruet. Hot glue bell to knot of bow.

2. Use glue stick to glue message to card stock; allow to dry. Use black marker to draw "stitches" around edges of message. Cut out tag as desired. Punch hole in tag. Use curling ribbon to attach tag to cruet.

VEGETABLE MEDLEY

Untie the bow,
Undo the pins,
Set the table,
Dinner begins!

Even if the weather is frightful, this garden-fresh dish is delightful! The casserole, which is a medley of vegetables topped with seasoned stuffing, will make taste buds sing with joy. For Yuletide flair, wrap your gift in holiday print place mats and tie with a rustic rope.

VEGETABLE CASSEROLE

Casserole can be made the day before and reheated to serve.

- $3/4$ cup chopped green pepper
- $3/4$ cup chopped onion
- 1 tablespoon butter or margarine
- 2 cans (15 ounces each) mixed vegetables, drained
- 2 cans ($15^1/4$ ounces each) whole kernel corn, drained
- 1 can (15 ounces) green peas, drained
- 1 container (8 ounces) sour cream
- $3/4$ cup mayonnaise
- 2 cups dry cornbread stuffing mix
- $1/2$ cup butter or margarine, melted
- $1/2$ cup grated Parmesan cheese

Preheat oven to 375 degrees. In a medium skillet, sauté green pepper and onion in 1 tablespoon butter until vegetables are translucent. Combine cooked vegetables and canned vegetables in a large bowl. Add sour cream and mayonnaise; stir until well blended. Spoon into a greased 9 x 13-inch baking dish. In a medium bowl, combine stuffing mix, melted butter, and cheese. Sprinkle topping over vegetable mixture. Bake about 25 minutes or until topping is golden and vegetables are heated through and bubbly. Serve warm or cover and store in refrigerator.

To reheat, place in a 375-degree oven about 45 minutes or until heated through.

Yield: about 16 servings

PLACE MAT-COVERED CASSEROLE DISH

You will need a casserole dish with lid (we used a 9" x 13" glass baking dish with rubber lid), two $13^1/2$" x $18^1/2$" fabric place mats, straight pins with ball heads, $2^2/3$ yds. of $1/2$" dia. jute rope, two 16" square fabric napkins, decorative-edge craft scissors, ecru card stock, black permanent fine-point marker, hole punch, and two 10" lengths of natural raffia.

1. Center covered dish on wrong side of one place mat. Center remaining place mat right side up on top of dish.
2. Bring long edges of bottom place mat up under long edges of top place mat; secure with pins. Fold short ends gift wrap style; secure with pins.
3. Beginning with center of rope across top of dish, wrap rope to bottom, twist rope at bottom, and bring ends to top of dish; tie ends into a bow. Fold napkins and place under bow.
4. For tag, use craft scissors to cut a $2^1/2$" x 4" piece from card stock. Use marker to write message on tag. Punch hole in corner of tag. Use raffia to attach tag to rope.

CREAMY CHRISTMAS COCOA

*H*elp friends take the chill off winter by presenting them with a jar of Almond Cocoa Mix. An ideal treat for anyone who enjoys warming up with a cup of hot cocoa, the delectable drink gets its creamy goodness from vanilla ice cream. Place a fabric-topped jar in a cheery mug for a quick, heartwarming gift.

ALMOND COCOA MIX

1   cup butter
1   cup granulated sugar
1   cup firmly packed brown sugar
2/3   cup cocoa
2   cups softened vanilla ice cream
2 1/2   teaspoons almond extract

In a medium saucepan, combine butter, sugars, and cocoa over low heat. Stirring frequently, cook until butter melts. Transfer mixture to a medium bowl. Add ice cream and almond extract; beat until smooth. Store in an airtight container in refrigerator. Give with storage and serving instructions.

Yield: about 4 cups cocoa mix

To serve: Store cocoa mix in refrigerator until ready to serve. Pour 3/4 cup boiling water or hot coffee over 1/4 cup cocoa mix; stir until well blended.

HOLLY JAR LID COVER

You will need a jar with lid, fabric, pinking shears, rubber band, green raffia, and an artificial holly sprig with berries.

1. Draw around jar lid on wrong side of fabric. Using pinking shears, cut out circle 2" outside drawn line.

2. Center fabric circle over jar lid; secure with rubber band. Knot several lengths of raffia around lid, covering rubber band. Insert holly under knot.

TOKENS OF CONFECTION

*K**ids** will love these novel party favors, and you won't have to worry about the "ice cream" melting — it's really frosting atop cupcakes baked right in the cones! Given in a cup wrapped in cellophane and tied with a festive bow, the cones make sweet tokens of "confection!"*

PARTY CUPCAKE CONES

These should be given the day they are made for maximum freshness of cones.

CUPCAKES

  1   package (18¼ ounces) white
       cake mix and ingredients to
       prepare cake
  1   tablespoon *each* green and red
       sprinkles
 25 small flat-bottom ice-cream cones

ICING

  5   cups confectioners sugar
 ¾   cup vegetable shortening
 ½   cup butter or margarine, softened
2½ to 3 tablespoons milk
1¼ teaspoons clear vanilla extract
      Peppermint candies

Preheat oven to 350 degrees. For cupcakes, prepare cake mix according to package directions, stirring in sprinkles. Fill each cone with about 2½ tablespoons batter. Place cones about 3 inches apart on an ungreased baking sheet. Bake 25 to 30 minutes or until a toothpick inserted in center of cupcake comes out clean. Cool completely.

For icing, combine confectioners sugar, shortening, butter, milk, and vanilla in a medium bowl; beat until smooth. Ice cupcakes. Place a candy on each cupcake. Let icing harden. Loosely cover with waxed paper.

Yield: 25 cupcakes

PARTY CUPCAKE BAGS

For each bag, you will need 22" of 1⅝"w red mesh ribbon, one white and one green chenille stem, two wrapped peppermint candies, 8 oz. clear plastic cup, and a 21" square of clear cellophane.

1. Fold mesh ribbon into a bow; twist green chenille stem around center of bow to secure. Twist green chenille stem around center of white chenille stem. Wrap each green stem end around a candy; curl green ends.
2. Place cone in cup; center cup on cellophane. Gather cellophane over cup; secure gathers with white stem.

SAVORY SOUP BASKET

Nothing can beat a bowl of steaming soup on a cold winter day! Our Lentil Soup Mix makes a welcome gift during the busy holidays — your friends can enjoy a hot, hearty meal without a lot of fuss. Deliver the "secret" seasoning mix, lentils, and cooking directions in a decorated basket that includes a pair of festive bowls!

LENTIL SOUP MIX

- 2 cups dried lentils
- 1 tablespoon chicken bouillon granules
- 1 tablespoon onion powder
- 1 teaspoon ground cumin
- 1 teaspoon celery salt
- 3/4 teaspoon salt
- 1/2 teaspoon garlic powder
- 1/2 teaspoon dried thyme leaves
- 1/2 teaspoon ground black pepper
- 1/4 teaspoon dried lemon peel
- 1 bay leaf

Place lentils in a resealable plastic bag. In a small bowl, combine chicken bouillon, onion powder, cumin, celery salt, salt, garlic powder, thyme, pepper, lemon peel, and bay leaf. Transfer seasoning mixture to a small cellophane bag. Give with serving instructions.

Yield: about 3 tablespoons seasoning mix

To serve: Rinse lentils. In a Dutch oven, cover lentils with 2 quarts water. Bring to a boil over medium-high heat. Reduce heat to medium low. Stirring occasionally, cover and simmer 15 minutes or until lentils are barely tender. Stir in seasoning mix. Cover and simmer 30 minutes longer or until lentils are tender. Serve warm.

Yield: about 7 cups soup

SOUP BOWL BASKET

You will need a 6¹/₂" x 22" piece of fabric, pinking shears, 12" of 1"w ribbon, 7" of ¹/₄"w ribbon, white card stock, black permanent fine-point marker, hole punch, two 5" lengths of ¹/₁₆"w satin ribbon, fabric for card, paper-backed fusible web, 3" x 5" plain index cards, hot glue gun, artificial berry garland, 10" dia. basket, natural excelsior, and two decorative soup bowls.

1. For fabric bag, matching right sides and short edges, fold fabric in half. Leaving a ¹/₄" seam allowance, sew sides of bag. Turn bag right side out. Trim top of bag with pinking shears. Place bag of lentils in fabric bag. Tie 1"w ribbon into a bow around top of bag.
2. Tie ¹/₄"w ribbon into a bow around top of seasoning mix bag.
3. For tags, cut two 1¹/₂" x 2" pieces from card stock. Use marker to write message on tags. Punch hole in corner of each tag; use ¹/₁₆"w ribbon to attach tags to bows.
4. For instruction card, cut one 1" x 3" piece each from fabric and web. Fuse web to fabric; fuse fabric to left side of index card. Use marker to write serving instructions on card.
5. Glue garland around rim of basket. Line basket with excelsior and place bags and bowls in basket.

"NACHO" ORDINARY POPCORN!

*T*his is not your ordinary popcorn! Flavorful cheese and spices will keep folks coming back for more Nacho Cheese Popcorn! Tossing it together is a snap, and our recipe makes plenty for sharing. A "recycled" Christmas card and a paper napkin make resourceful trims for a bucket full of your tasty treats.

NACHO CHEESE POPCORN

20 cups popped popcorn
¹/₂ cup butter or margarine, melted
1 envelope (1¹/₄ ounces) cheese sauce mix
1 tablespoon Worcestershire sauce
2 teaspoons chili powder
1 teaspoon garlic salt
¹/₄ teaspoon ground red pepper

Preheat oven to 250 degrees. Place popcorn in a greased large roasting pan; set aside. In a small bowl, combine butter, cheese sauce mix, Worcestershire sauce, chili powder, garlic salt, and red pepper. Drizzle butter mixture over popcorn; stir until well coated. Bake 30 minutes, stirring every 10 minutes. Spread on aluminum foil to cool. Store in an airtight container.

Yield: about 17 cups popcorn

CHRISTMAS BUCKET

You will need a printed paper napkin, rectangular galvanized bucket with a handle (we used an 8" x 11¹/₂" bucket with a 1¹/₂"w handle), spray adhesive, 1"w grosgrain ribbon, craft glue,

Christmas card, and card stock to coordinate with card.

1. Unfold and press napkin. Separate napkin into layers.
2. Using printed layer of napkin only, place bucket front side down on wrong side of napkin. Draw around bucket. Cutting 1" outside drawn line, cut shape from napkin. Apply spray adhesive to wrong side of napkin piece; center and smooth onto front of bucket. Trim sides of napkin even with sides of bucket. Smooth excess napkin to inside and bottom of bucket.

3. Measure height of bucket; add 2". Cut two lengths of ribbon the determined measurement. Center and glue one ribbon length along each side on front of bucket, covering sides of napkin. Glue excess ribbon to inside and bottom of bucket. Measure length of handle. Cut a length of ribbon the determined measurement. Glue ribbon to handle.
4. Cut desired motif from Christmas card. Glue to card stock. Leaving a ¹/₄" card stock border, cut out motif. Center and glue motif to front of bucket.

JUST POPPIN' IN

When you pop in to say "Merry Christmas" to the popcorn lovers on your gift list, be sure to take some popping corn and our Microwave Popcorn Seasoning Mix. The savory topping, made with seasonings you'll find in the cupboard, offers an easy way to spice up a piping hot bag of their favorite snack.

MICROWAVE POPCORN SEASONING MIX

- 1/2 cup freshly grated Parmesan cheese
- 1 teaspoon paprika
- 1 teaspoon dried Italian herb seasoning
- 1/2 teaspoon garlic powder
- 1/4 teaspoon ground red pepper
- 8 bags (3 1/2 ounces each) unpopped microwave popcorn

In a small bowl, combine Parmesan cheese, paprika, Italian seasoning, garlic powder, and red pepper until well blended. Place 1 tablespoon seasoning mix in each of 8 small plastic bags. Store in refrigerator. Give 1 bag of popcorn and serving instructions with each bag of seasoning mix.

Yield: about 1/2 cup seasoning mix

To serve: Microwave a 3 1/2-ounce bag of microwave popcorn according to package directions. Open bag carefully to avoid steam. Sprinkle seasoning mix (1 tablespoon) over popcorn; hold top of bag closed and shake until popcorn is coated.

SANTA POPCORN PACKETS

For each packet, you will need decorative-edge craft scissors; lunch-size brown paper bag; packet of microwave popcorn; natural, red, and green raffia; photocopy of Santa label (page 113) and holly design (page 112) on ecru card stock; colored pencils; and a hot glue gun.

1. Use craft scissors to trim top of bag. Place popcorn and seasoning mix in flat bag. Wrap top of bag around popcorn and seasoning mix. Knot several lengths of raffia around packet to secure.

2. Use craft scissors to cut out Santa label and holly design 1/4" outside outer lines. Use pencils to color label and holly design. Glue holly design over knot of raffia and Santa label to opposite side of packet.

HEAVENLY LEMON BARS

*T*art and sweet, Lemon-Pecan Bars appeal to the most discriminating tastes! Using our almost effortless recipe, you can bake these elegant delights in no time. Be ready for special guests by boxing the bars in pretty appliquéd boxes.

LEMON-PECAN BARS

CRUST

- 2 cups all-purpose flour
- 1/2 cup confectioners sugar
- 3/4 cup chilled butter or margarine, cut into pieces
- 3/4 cup chopped pecans, toasted and coarsely ground

FILLING

- 2 cups sugar
- 4 eggs
- 1/3 cup freshly squeezed lemon juice
- 1/4 cup all-purpose flour
- 1/2 teaspoon baking powder
- 1 cup chopped pecans, toasted

Preheat oven to 350 degrees. For crust, combine flour and confectioners sugar in a medium bowl. Using a pastry blender or 2 knives, cut in butter until mixture resembles coarse meal. Stir in pecans. Press dough into bottom and 1/4 inch up sides of a greased 9 x 13-inch baking pan. Bake 20 minutes.

For filling, combine sugar, eggs, and lemon juice in a large bowl; whisk until well blended. In a small bowl, combine flour and baking powder. Add dry ingredients to sugar mixture; whisk until well blended. Stir in pecans. Pour mixture into warm crust. Bake 25 to 30 minutes longer or until filling is set. Cool in pan. Cut into 1 x 2-inch bars. Store in an airtight container in refrigerator.

Yield: about 4 dozen bars

ANGEL BOX

You will need a 6 1/2" x 8" oval Shaker box with lid, red acrylic paint, paintbrush, paper-backed fusible web, muslin, fabric scraps for appliqués, craft glue, hot glue gun, 24" of 5/8"w green grosgrain ribbon, seven assorted buttons, brown dimensional paint, pink colored pencil, and a brown permanent fine-point marker.

1. Remove lid from box. Paint outside of box red; allow to dry.
2. Draw around lid on paper side of web; cut out oval. To mark center of oval, fold oval in half lengthwise; draw along crease on paper side of web. Draw a horizontal line across oval 3 5/8" from each end. Fuse oval to muslin; do not remove paper backing.
3. Using patterns, page 114, follow *Making Appliqués*, page 121, to make head, body, wings, large star, tree, six small stars, two 1 1/4" x 3 3/4", and two 3" x 3 1/2" appliqués.
4. Arrange small stars around side of box; fuse in place. Using lines drawn on oval web as guide, arrange and fuse remaining appliqués on muslin.
5. Cut out muslin oval 1/2" outside edge of web. Clip edges of fabric oval at 1/2" intervals to 1/8" from edge of web. Center and fuse oval on box lid.
6. Using craft glue, glue clipped edges to side of lid. Covering clipped edges, hot glue ribbon around side of lid. Hot glue one button to center of each star.
7. For angel, use dimensional paint to paint dots for hair, pink pencil to color cheeks, and marker to make dots for eyes.
8. Use marker to draw "stitches" along edges of stars and muslin areas.

ZESTY BAGEL SPREAD

Give your favorite bagel lover something to smile about this Christmas. A package of Savory Herb Bagel Mix, when blended with softened cream cheese, will add flavor to the holidays. Fuse cheery checked fabric to poster board to create the wraparound packet; finish by tying on a handy cheese spreader.

SAVORY HERB BAGEL MIX

1	cup dried parsley flakes
1/3	cup dried dill weed
2 1/2	tablespoons dried oregano leaves
2 1/2	tablespoons dried thyme leaves
2	tablespoons salt
4	teaspoons dried rosemary leaves
4	teaspoons dried marjoram leaves
2	teaspoons paprika

Combine all ingredients in a resealable plastic bag. Give with serving instructions.

Yield: about 2 cups mix

To serve: Process 2 teaspoons mix with one 8-ounce package softened cream cheese in a food processor until smooth. Transfer to an airtight container. Chill 2 hours to let flavors blend. Serve spread on bagel slices.

Yield: about 1 cup spread

BAGEL SPREAD PACKETS

For each packet, you will need one 6" x 15" piece each of white poster board, fabric, and paper-backed fusible web; stapler; hole punch; two 15" lengths of 1/4"w grosgrain ribbon; hot glue gun; decorative spreader; photocopy of label design (page 115) on white card stock; spray adhesive; and green card stock.

1. Fuse fabric to poster board.
2. Fold one end of poster board 6 1/2" to wrong side. Staple bag of seasoning mix to wrong side of folded end. For flap, fold opposite end of poster board 2" to wrong side. Punch two holes 1/2" apart in center of flap. Thread ribbons through holes. Fold packet and glue flap to secure.
3. Tie ribbons into a bow around spreader.
4. For label, cut out label design. Apply spray adhesive to wrong side of label design; smooth onto green card stock. Leaving a 1/8" green border, cut out label. Apply spray adhesive to wrong side of label; center and smooth onto packet.

"A-PEEL-ING" GOODNESS

Create an "a-peel-ing" gift for a special teacher — or anyone who enjoys the natural goodness of fruit. To complete this A+ offering, pack a serving of the mix in a paper bag, tie with a raffia bow, and place in a beribboned basket filled with bright red apples. A festive cross-stitched hand towel adds a nice touch.

TASTY FRUIT DIP MIX

1 cup firmly packed brown sugar

3 tablespoons chopped crystallized ginger

2 teaspoons ground cinnamon
Apples to give

Process brown sugar, ginger, and cinnamon in a food processor until ginger is finely chopped. Store in an airtight container. Give with apples and serving instructions.

Yield: about 1¼ cups mix

To serve: In a small bowl, beat 3 tablespoons mix into one 8-ounce package softened cream cheese until well blended. Cover and chill 1 hour to let flavors blend. Serve with pieces of fruit.

Yield: about 1 cup spread

HOLIDAY BASKET ENSEMBLE

You will need embroidery floss (see color key, page 115), white fingertip towel with 2½"w border of Aida (14 ct), basket (we used a 9" dia. basket with handle), fabric for basket trim, hot glue gun, 3" x 6" brown paper bag, hole punch, several 8" lengths of natural raffia, red

and black permanent fine-point markers, and 2" x 2½" piece of white card stock for label.

Refer to Cross Stitch, page 123, before beginning project.

1. Using three strands of floss for *Cross Stitch* and one strand of floss for *Backstitch*, stitch design, page 115, on towel.

2. Measure around rim of basket; add ½". Measure height of rim; add ½". Cut a strip from fabric the determined

measurements. Press each long edge of fabric strip ¼" to wrong side. Overlapping ends at back, glue fabric around rim of basket.

3. For gift bag, place gift in bag. Fold top of bag 1" to front twice. Punch two holes 1" apart in center of folded portion of bag. Thread raffia through holes; tie into a bow at front of bag.

4. Use black marker to write message on label. Use red marker to draw dots and dashes along edges of label. Glue label to bag.

THE PROOF'S IN THE PUDDING

*T*he proof is in the pudding — these cookies are chock-full of flavor! We used three pudding mixes (chocolate, butterscotch, and lemon) and a variety of flavored chips with one basic recipe to create a trio of yummy Pudding Cookies. Set them out for Santa, or give them as hostess gifts.

PUDDING COOKIES

We made 3 separate cookie recipes for 3 different flavors.

    1   cup butter or margarine, softened
  $^1/_2$ cup granulated sugar
  $^1/_2$ cup firmly packed brown sugar
    2   eggs
    2   teaspoons vanilla extract
  $2^1/_2$ cups all-purpose flour
    1   teaspoon baking soda
  $^1/_4$ teaspoon salt

Preheat oven to 350 degrees. In a large bowl, cream butter and sugars until fluffy. Add eggs and vanilla; beat until smooth. In a medium bowl, combine flour, baking soda, salt, and ingredients from one of the variations. Add dry ingredients to creamed mixture; stir until a soft dough forms. Drop by tablespoonfuls onto a lightly greased baking sheet. Bake 9 to 11 minutes or until bottoms are lightly browned. Transfer cookies to a wire rack to cool. Store in an airtight container.

Yield: about 4 dozen cookies

CHOCOLATE: 3.9-ounce package chocolate instant pudding mix and 6-ounce package semisweet chocolate chips

BUTTERSCOTCH: 3.4-ounce package butterscotch instant pudding mix and $7^1/_2$-ounce package almond brickle chips

LEMON: 3.4-ounce package lemon instant pudding mix and 10-ounce package raspberry-flavored semisweet chocolate chips

HEART TAGS

For each tag, you will need a wooden heart, yellow card stock, craft glue, black permanent fine-point marker, 5" of jute twine, hot glue gun, and a $^1/_2$" dia. button.

1. Draw around wooden heart on card stock; cut out $^1/_4$" inside drawn line. Use craft glue to glue card stock heart to wooden heart; allow to dry. Use marker to write message on tag.
2. Fold twine in half. Hot glue ends to front of heart. Hot glue button over twine.

IRRESISTIBLE PRALINES

*S*imple *to whip up using pudding mix, Easy But Rich Pralines are irresistible sweets! Package small batches in handcrafted nutcracker bags created from brown paper sacks and scraps of craft materials. They make great gifts for surprise holiday visitors.*

EASY BUT RICH PRALINES

- 1 cup firmly packed brown sugar
- 1/2 cup granulated sugar
- 1 package (3 ounces) vanilla pudding mix
- 1 can (5 ounces) evaporated milk
- 1 tablespoon butter or margarine
- 1 1/2 cups chopped pecans

In a heavy large saucepan, combine sugars, pudding mix, evaporated milk, and butter. Stirring frequently, bring to a boil over medium heat; stir in pecans. Attach a candy thermometer to pan, making sure thermometer does not touch bottom of pan. Cook, stirring occasionally, until mixture reaches 234 degrees. Test about 1/2 teaspoon mixture in ice water. Mixture will easily form a ball in ice water but will flatten when removed from water. Remove from heat; beat 2 to 3 minutes or until mixture begins to thicken. Working quickly, drop tablespoonfuls of candy onto waxed paper; let cool. Store in an airtight container.

Yield: about 2 dozen pralines

NUTCRACKER GIFT BAG

You will need a lunch-size brown paper bag; 2 1/2"w ribbon; low-temperature glue gun; tracing paper; peach, red, and blue craft foam; white artificial fur; red permanent medium-point marker; 3/4" x 1 1/8" piece of white poster board; two 5/8" dia. black buttons; and a 3/4" dia. yellow button.

1. Measure width of front of bag. Cut a length of ribbon the determined measurement. Glue ribbon across bottom on front of bag.
2. Trace patterns, page 116, onto tracing

paper; cut out. Using patterns, cut nose from peach craft foam, crown and two cheeks from red craft foam, and hatband from blue craft foam. Cutting through fabric backing only, cut mustache, beard, and two eyebrows from fur. Use marker to draw teeth on poster board piece.
3. Fold top of bag 1 1/2" to back. Overlapping as necessary, arrange and glue foam shapes, fur shapes, and teeth on bag. Glue black buttons to bag for eyes and yellow button to top of crown.
4. Unfold top of bag. Place gift in bag. Refold top of bag; glue to secure.

"LOAFING" AROUND

There's no time for loafing around during the holidays — unless you're baking some of our Banana-Crunch Loaves! The moist, fruity sweet bread gets its crispy goodness from a candied topping packed with pecans. The miniature loaves are delivered with cross-stitched gift tags, which can be used as tree trimmers.

BANANA-CRUNCH LOAVES

CANDIED PECAN TOPPING

- 2 egg whites
- 1/2 cup firmly packed brown sugar
- 1 teaspoon ground cinnamon
- 1 teaspoon vanilla extract
- 1/8 teaspoon salt
- 3 cups chopped pecans

CAKE

- 1/2 cup butter or margarine, softened
- 1/2 cup shortening
- 2 3/4 cups sugar
- 4 eggs
- 2 egg yolks
- 1 1/4 cups mashed bananas (about 3 medium bananas)
- 1 1/2 teaspoons vanilla extract
- 3 cups all-purpose flour
- 1/4 teaspoon baking powder
- 1/4 teaspoon baking soda
- 1 cup buttermilk

For candied pecan topping, beat egg whites in a medium bowl until soft peaks form. In a small bowl, combine brown sugar, cinnamon, vanilla, and salt; beat into egg whites. Fold in pecans; set aside.

Preheat oven to 325 degrees. For cake, cream butter, shortening, and sugar in a large bowl until fluffy. Add eggs and egg yolks, 1 at a time, beating well after each addition. Beat in bananas and vanilla.

In a medium bowl, combine flour, baking powder, and baking soda. Alternately beat dry ingredients and buttermilk into batter, beating until well blended. Spoon into 8 greased 3 x 5 3/4-inch loaf pans.

Spoon pecan topping over batter. Bake 50 to 60 minutes or until a toothpick inserted in center of loaf comes out clean. Cool in pans 10 minutes. Remove from pans and cool completely on a wire rack. Store in an airtight container.

Yield: about 8 loaves

CROSS-STITCHED TAGS

For each tag, you will need embroidery floss (see color key, page 103), 4" square of white perforated plastic (14 ct), craft glue, 3" of gold cord, and green card stock.

Refer to Cross Stitch, page 123, before beginning project.

1. Using three strands of floss for *Cross Stitch* and one strand of floss for *Backstitch,* center and stitch design, page 103, on perforated plastic. Leaving one stitch width for border, cut out design.
2. For hanger, glue ends of cord to back of design. Glue design to card stock; allow to dry. Leaving a 1/8" green border, cut out tag.

UNBEATABLE TREAT

A delight for the taste buds, this Toasted Pecan-Pepper Jam offers a sweet yet subtly tangy flavor. Trim a jar of the jam with fabric and naturals, then place in a basket along with crackers and a package of cream cheese for a treat that can't be beat!

TOASTED PECAN-PEPPER JAM

- 3 cups chopped sweet red peppers
- ¹/₂ cup apple cider vinegar
- 1 package (1³/₄ ounces) powdered fruit pectin
- 4¹/₂ cups sugar
- 1 cup finely chopped pecans, toasted
  Crackers to serve

Process peppers in a food processor until finely chopped. In a Dutch oven, combine peppers, vinegar, and pectin over medium-high heat. Bring to a rolling boil. Add sugar. Stirring constantly, bring to a rolling boil again and boil 1 minute. Stir in pecans. Remove from heat; skim off foam. Spoon jam into heat-resistant jars; cover and cool to room temperature. Store in refrigerator. Serve with crackers.

Yield: about 5¹/₂ cups jam

RUSTIC BASKET

You will need fabric, rubber band, wired artificial pine greenery, pinecone, hot glue gun, basket (we used a 7¹/₂" x 10¹/₂" oval birch-bark basket), and shredded paper.

1. For jar lid cover, measure across jar lid; add 4". Tear a square from fabric the

determined measurement. Center fabric over lid; secure with rubber band.
2. Measure around jar lid; add 2". Cut a length of greenery the determined measurement. Covering rubber band, wrap greenery around lid; twist ends together to secure. Glue pinecone over twist of greenery.
3. Line basket with shredded paper. Place jar and a bag of crackers in basket.

CANDIED APPLE PIE

Fresh-baked goodies are always great gifts, and they're especially appreciated around the holidays. Our Candied Apple Pie is a new twist on America's favorite dessert — it captures the sweet, cinnamony taste of candied apples in a pie! Add a holly sprig to a cheery bow to decorate your pie carrier.

CANDIED APPLE PIE

CRUST

- 2 cups all-purpose flour
- 1 teaspoon salt
- 3/4 cup vegetable shortening
- 6 to 8 tablespoons cold water

FILLING

- 1/4 cup butter or margarine
- 7 cups peeled, cored, and sliced Rome apples (about 6 medium apples)
- 1 cup sugar
- 1/2 cup small red cinnamon candies
- 2 tablespoons water
  Whipping cream
  White coarse decorating sugar

For crust, combine flour and salt in a small bowl. Using a pastry blender or 2 knives, cut in shortening until mixture resembles coarse meal. Sprinkle with water; mix until a soft dough forms. Divide dough in half. On a lightly floured surface, use a floured rolling pin to roll out half of dough into a 12-inch circle. Transfer dough to a 9-inch pie plate and use a sharp knife to trim edge of dough. Roll out remaining half of dough into a 12-inch circle, cover with plastic wrap.

Preheat oven to 425 degrees. For filling, melt butter in a large skillet over medium heat. Add apples, sugar, candies, and water. Stirring frequently, cook about 25 minutes or until juice thickens and apples are tender. Transfer apple mixture to a heatproof container; cool 15 minutes.

Spoon apple mixture into pie crust. Using a fluted pastry wheel, cut remaining dough into 1 1/4-inch-wide strips. Arrange strips lattice-style on top of pie. Crimp edges of pie with a fork. Lightly brush pastry with whipping cream. Sprinkle with decorating sugar. Bake 25 to 30 minutes or until crust is golden brown. If edge of crust browns too quickly, cover with a strip of aluminum foil. Serve warm or cool completely. Store in an airtight container.

Yield: about 8 servings

DECORATED PIE CARRIER

You will need 18" of 2 1/2"w wired ribbon, pie carrier (we used an 8 1/2" dia. wire pie carrier with wooden handles), hot glue gun, artificial greenery (we used a stem of holly leaves with berries), self-adhesive gift tag, red paper, decorative-edge craft scissors, black permanent fine-point marker, hole punch, and 5" of 1/8"w satin ribbon.

1. Tie wired ribbon into a bow around wire of one handle on pie carrier.
2. Glue greenery to knot of bow.
3. For tag, apply gift tag to red paper. Leaving a 1/8" red border, use craft scissors to cut out tag. Use marker to write message on tag.
4. Punch hole in corner of tag; use satin ribbon to attach tag to bow.

FANTASTIC FUDGE

Satisfy a friend's craving for sweets with a tin of tantalizing treats! Caramel-Pecan Fudge features a creamy-smooth fudge layer covered by a crunchy-sweet topping. A decorative tin — tied with ribbon and embellished with a chenille bow and a star cutout — makes a stellar gift box.

CARAMEL-PECAN FUDGE

FUDGE

- 4 cups sugar
- 1 cup evaporated milk
- 1/2 cup dark corn syrup
- 6 tablespoons butter or margarine
- 1 teaspoon vanilla extract

TOPPING

- 1 cup sugar
- 1/4 cup water
- 1/4 cup butter
- 2 tablespoons evaporated milk
- 1 teaspoon vanilla extract
- 1 cup chopped pecans, toasted

For fudge, butter sides of a heavy large saucepan. Combine sugar, evaporated milk, corn syrup, and butter in pan. Stirring constantly, cook over medium-low heat until sugar dissolves. Using a pastry brush dipped in hot water, wash down any sugar crystals on sides of pan. Attach a candy thermometer to pan, making sure thermometer does not touch bottom of pan. Increase heat to medium and bring to a boil. Cook, without stirring, until mixture reaches soft-ball stage (approximately 234 to 240 degrees). Test about 1/2 teaspoon mixture in ice water. Mixture will easily form a ball in ice water

but will flatten when removed from water. Place pan in 2 inches of cold water in sink. Add vanilla; do not stir. Cool to approximately 110 degrees. Remove from sink. Using medium speed of an electric mixer, beat until fudge thickens and begins to lose its gloss. Pour into 2 greased 3-cup decorative tins.

For topping, combine sugar and water in a heavy small skillet. Swirling occasionally, cook over medium-high heat until sugar dissolves. Increase heat to high. Swirling frequently, cook until mixture turns golden. Remove from heat (syrup will be very hot). Carefully add butter; stir until melted. Gradually stir in evaporated milk and vanilla. Stir in pecans. Pour topping over fudge; let cool. Cover tins and store in a cool place.

Yield: 2 tins fudge, about 1²/₃ pounds each tin

TIN WITH BOW AND TAG

You will need ³/₄"w ribbon, decorative tin (we used a 9¹/₂" x 4" x 1¹/₄"h tin), silver tinsel stem, silver thread, and a purchased star tag.

1. Measure around tin length and width; add 20". Cut ribbon the determined length. Beginning with center of ribbon across top of tin, wrap ribbon to bottom, twist ribbon at bottom, and bring ends to top of tin; knot at center.
2. Twist tinsel stem into a bow; position on top of ribbon knot. Tie ribbon into a bow around tinsel stem bow.
3. Use thread to attach star to bow.

Just Desserts

*I*f someone on your gift list deserves a special treat, reward them with a Cranberry-Orange Pie. The creamy filling is poured into a ready-made graham cracker crust, so it's extra-easy to prepare. For a sweet delivery, we wrapped a pie in cellophane and decorated it with a striped bow and a handmade ornament.

CRANBERRY-ORANGE PIES

- 1 container (8 ounces) frozen non-dairy whipped topping, thawed and divided
- 1 can (14 ounces) sweetened condensed milk
- 1 can (6 ounces) frozen cranberry juice cocktail concentrate, thawed
- 3/4 cup whole berry cranberry sauce
- 1/4 teaspoon orange extract
- 2 purchased graham cracker pie crusts (6 ounces each)

Place 1 cup whipped topping in a small bowl; set aside. Beat sweetened condensed milk, cranberry juice concentrate, cranberry sauce, and orange extract in a large bowl with an electric mixer until well blended. Fold in remaining whipped topping. Spoon into crusts. Spoon reserved whipped topping into a pastry bag fitted with a large star tip. Pipe topping onto each pie. Cover with plastic lids and store in freezer. Serve chilled.

Yield: 2 pies, 8 servings each

ORANGE SLICE ORNAMENT

You will need tracing paper, corrugated paper, poster board, hot glue gun, preserved evergreen, cinnamon sticks, dried orange slice, hole punch, and 6" of string.

1. Trace star pattern, page 117, onto tracing paper; cut out. Using pattern, cut one star each from corrugated paper and poster board. Glue corrugated paper star to poster board star. Glue evergreen, cinnamon sticks, and dried orange slice to star.

2. For hanger, punch a hole in top of star. Thread string through hole; knot ends 2" from ornament.

HOLIDAY MUNCHIES

*W*rap up a friend's holiday snacking with a jar of Caramelized Peanuts. The nutty-sweet goodness is great anytime! We placed a pint-size jar of the crunchy snack in a cloth napkin and finished with a star-studded napkin ring and handmade gift tag.

CARAMELIZED PEANUTS

1 cup sugar
1/2 cup water
1 can (12 ounces) Spanish peanuts

Butter sides of a heavy medium skillet. Combine sugar and water in skillet. Stirring constantly, cook over medium-high heat until sugar dissolves. Bring to a boil; cook, without stirring, until sugar is golden brown (about 10 minutes), swirling skillet occasionally. Add peanuts; stir until coated. Remove from heat and spread on greased aluminum foil to cool. Break into pieces. Store in an airtight container.

Yield: about 4 cups peanuts

NAPKIN-COVERED JAR

You will need a pint-size jar with lid, 17" square red fabric napkin, rubber band, napkin ring (we used a ring with a brass star), self-adhesive gift tag, white card stock, decorative-edge craft scissors, hole punch, and 5" of gold cord.

1. Center jar on wrong side of napkin. Gather napkin over jar and secure gathers with rubber band; cover rubber band with napkin ring.

2. For tag, apply gift tag to card stock. Leaving a 1/8" white border, use craft scissors to cut out tag.

3. Punch hole in tag. Use cord to tie tag to napkin ring.

"SOUP-ER" FARE

*C*hase away winter chills by giving your friends a jar of Beer-Cheese Soup. A piping hot bowl of this creamy stock will warm the heart as well as the body! Festive wrapping paper and curling ribbon transform an ordinary canister into a "soup-er" container.

BEER-CHEESE SOUP

- 2 cans (10¾ ounces each) cream of potato soup
- 2 cans (10¾ ounces each) Cheddar cheese soup
- 1 jar (2 ounces) diced pimiento
- 2 teaspoons dried minced onion
- 2 teaspoons dried parsley flakes
- ¼ teaspoon ground red pepper
- 2 cups milk
- 1 can (12 ounces) beer
- 1 package (8 ounces) shredded sharp Cheddar cheese

In a Dutch oven over medium heat, combine soups, pimiento, onion, parsley flakes, and red pepper; stir until well blended. Stir in milk, beer, and cheese. Stirring occasionally, cook until heated through and smooth (about 15 minutes). Serve warm. Store in an airtight container in refrigerator.

Yield: about 10 cups soup

COVERED CANISTER

You will need a canister with lid (we used a 2-quart acrylic canister with wire-hinged lid), poster board, Christmas-motif wrapping paper, spray adhesive, hot glue gun, several 1 yd. lengths of curling ribbon, and white card stock.

1. Measure around canister; add ½". Measure height of canister between rim and bottom of canister. Cut one piece each from poster board and wrapping paper the determined measurements.
2. Apply spray adhesive to wrong side of wrapping paper; smooth paper onto poster board. Wrap poster board around canister; glue to secure.
3. Tie ribbons into a bow around canister; curl ribbon ends.
4. For tag, cut desired motif from wrapping paper. Apply spray adhesive to wrong side of motif; smooth motif onto card stock. Leaving a ⅛" card stock border, cut out tag. Apply spray adhesive to wrong side of tag; center and smooth on lid.

Almond-flavored liqueur adds punch to luscious Amaretto Baklava — a traditional Greek pastry made with honey and nuts. Our version includes a fruity helping of peach preserves, along with a generous portion of toasted almonds. An embellished tulle wrap gives an ordinary aluminum pan a touch of sophistication.

AMARETTO BAKLAVA

1 1/2 cups sugar, divided
1/2 cup water
1/2 cup honey
3 tablespoons amaretto, divided
1/2 teaspoon almond extract
2 cups slivered almonds, toasted and coarsely ground
1/2 cup peach preserves
1/8 teaspoon ground nutmeg
1 package (16 ounces) frozen phyllo pastry, thawed
1 cup butter, melted

In a small saucepan, combine 1 cup sugar, water, and honey. Stirring constantly, bring to a boil over medium heat. Reduce heat to low. Stirring frequently, simmer 10 minutes. Remove from heat and stir in 2 tablespoons amaretto and almond extract; set aside. In a medium bowl, combine almonds, preserves, remaining 1/2 cup sugar, remaining 1 tablespoon amaretto, and nutmeg. Stir until well blended; set aside.

Preheat oven to 350 degrees. Cut pastry in half crosswise (sheets will measure about 8 1/2 x 12 inches). Keep pastry covered with plastic wrap and a damp towel. Grease two 8-inch square aluminum foil cake pans (with plastic lids). Brushing each pastry sheet with melted butter, place 1 sheet in each pan, gently fitting into bottom of pan and allowing ends to hang over sides of pans. Place a second sheet opposite the first to form a cross. Continue layering in this manner for a total of 6 sheets in each pan. Press 1/2 cup almond mixture over pastry in each pan. Repeat process using another layer of pastry (6 sheets) and almond mixture, ending with a third layer of pastry. Use a very sharp knife to score top layer of pastry into diamond-shaped pieces. Fold in edges of pastry to fit pan and form a rim. Gently brush surface with melted butter. Bake 25 to 30 minutes or until golden brown. Drizzle sugar mixture over warm baklava. Cool completely in pans. Using scored lines, cut into pieces to serve. Cover pans with plastic lids.

Yield: about 2 dozen pieces each pan

SILVER-WRAPPED PAN

You will need a 28" square of decorative tulle (we used white with silver threads), white chenille stem, hot glue gun, glittered white artificial floral sprig with berries, 24" of white curling ribbon, and a purchased gift tag.

1. Center pan on tulle. Gather tulle over pan; secure gathers with chenille stem. Glue sprig to gathers.
2. Use ribbon to attach tag to gift; curl ribbon ends.

FUN CHRISTMAS TREES

*W*e'll let you decide which is more fun — making these jolly Christmas tree treats or eating them! Created using a packaged cake mix, the "trees" are glazed with green icing and then trimmed with red "garlands" and candy sprinkles. Peppermint sticks form the "trunks."

FUN CHRISTMAS TREES

CAKE

1 package (18¼ ounces) white cake mix with pudding in the mix and ingredients to prepare cake
 Green paste food coloring

GREEN ICING

4 cups confectioners sugar
5 to 6 tablespoons half and half
1 teaspoon vanilla extract
 Green paste food coloring

RED ICING

1 cup confectioners sugar
1 to 2 tablespoons half and half
½ teaspoon vanilla extract
 Red paste food coloring
 Multicolored non-pareils
 Peppermint candy sticks or candy canes

Trace pattern, page 120, onto stencil plastic; cut out. Preheat oven to 350 degrees. For cake, grease a 10½ by 15½-inch jellyroll pan. Line bottom with waxed paper; grease waxed paper. Mix cake according to package directions; tint batter green. Pour into prepared pan. Bake 18 to 20 minutes or until a

toothpick inserted in center of cake comes out clean. Cool in pan. Invert cake onto a large cutting board. Cut cake lengthwise into thirds (each piece should measure about 3¼ x 14 inches). Use pattern to cut 9 tree-shaped cakes from each section. Place cakes on a wire rack with waxed paper underneath.

For green icing, combine confectioners sugar, half and half, and vanilla in a medium bowl; stir until smooth. Tint green.

For red icing, combine confectioners sugar, half and half, and vanilla in a small bowl; stir until smooth. Tint red. Spoon icing into a pastry bag fitted with a small round tip.

To decorate cakes, spoon green icing over tops of cakes. While icing is still wet, pipe red "garland" onto cakes. Sprinkle some of the cakes with non-pareils. Let icing harden. Store in an airtight container in a single layer. When ready to give, insert a peppermint stick into bottom of each cake for "tree trunk."

Yield: 27 cakes

84

HOLIDAY STARS

These taste-tempting truffles will quickly become holiday stars. By melting the chocolate and butterscotch chips in the microwave, you can make rich confections for all the sweets lovers on your list, and still have time for entertaining! Wrap a star-shaped plate of trufffles with cellophane and tie with ribbon and an ornament for a dazzling delivery.

EASY TRUFFLES

- 1 package (6 ounces) semisweet chocolate chips
- 1 cup butterscotch chips
- 3/4 cup confectioners sugar
- 1/2 cup sour cream
- 2 teaspoons grated orange zest
- 1/4 teaspoon salt
- 1 package (11 ounces) vanilla wafers, finely crushed
  Confectioners sugar

In a medium microwave-safe bowl, microwave chips on medium power (50%) until chips soften, stirring frequently until smooth. Stir in 3/4 cup confectioners sugar, sour cream, orange zest, salt, and wafer crumbs. Shape mixture into 1-inch balls. Roll in confectioners sugar. Store in an airtight container in refrigerator.

Yield: about 5 dozen balls

STARRY PLATE

For each plate, you will need an 8"w decorative plate (we used a silver star-shaped plate), 30" square of clear cellophane, 24" each of 5/8"w red satin

and 7/8"w white sheer ribbon, two 24" lengths of silver cord, white and red card stock, decorative-edge craft scissors, spray adhesive, red permanent fine-point marker, hole punch, and an ornament with hanger.

1. Arrange truffles on plate. Place plate on center of cellophane. Gather cellophane over top of plate; tie ribbons and one length of cord into a bow around gathers.

2. For tag, cut a 1 3/4" x 2 1/2" piece from red card stock. Use craft scissors to cut a 1 1/4" x 2" piece from white card stock. Apply spray adhesive to one side of white card stock; smooth white card stock onto red card stock.

3. Use marker to write message on tag. Punch a hole in one corner of tag. Use remaining length of cord to tie tag and ornament to gift.

LEMON SIZZLE

*B*ecause our Lemon-Pepper Basting Sauce is bursting with citrusy flavor, it's no lemon of a gift! The easy-to-make condiment is great on chicken or fish. Include a decorative oven mitt and basting brush with the sauce for a gift that's guaranteed to sizzle!

LEMON-PEPPER BASTING SAUCE

- 1 cup mayonnaise
- 1/2 cup freshly squeezed lemon juice
- 1 tablespoon lemon pepper

In a small bowl, combine mayonnaise, lemon juice, and lemon pepper. Store in an airtight container in refrigerator. Give with serving instructions.

Yield: about 1 1/2 cups sauce

To serve: Brush pieces of chicken or fish with sauce before baking, broiling, or grilling.

DECORATED SAUCE JAR

You will need fabric, paper-backed fusible web, 2 1/2" x 4 1/2" piece of red card stock, decorative-edge craft scissors, red permanent fine-point marker, 1 1/2" x 3" piece of white card stock, craft glue, felt, pint-size jar with lid and band, and 3/8"w satin ribbon.

1. For label, cut one 2" x 4 1/2" piece each from fabric and fusible web. Fuse web to wrong side of fabric; fuse fabric to red card stock. Use craft scissors to trim

edges of red card stock. Use marker to draw border along edges and write message on white card stock. Glue white card stock to label and glue label to jar; allow to dry.

2. For jar lid insert, use fabric and follow *Jar Lid Finishing*, page 122, to cover lid. Measure around jar band; add 15". Cut a piece of ribbon the determined length. Tie ribbon into a bow around band.

COFFEE & TEA TIME

Any time is the right time for a cup of coffee or hot tea flavored with these delicious mixes. The taste of rich hazelnut creamer or cherry-flavored sugar is sure to delight! Create a cute gift basket by adding a fabric napkin, a jar of mix, and some coffee or tea bags. For a final touch, embellish the basket with ribbons and greenery.

RICH HAZELNUT COFFEE CREAMER

- 1 jar (8 ounces) hazelnut-flavored non-dairy powdered creamer
- 2 tablespoons cocoa
- 1 teaspoon vanilla-butter-nut flavoring

Process creamer and cocoa in a small food processor until blended. Sprinkle vanilla-butter-nut flavoring over creamer mixture; process until well blended. Store in an airtight container in a cool place. Give with serving instructions.

Yield: about 1²/₃ cups creamer

To serve: Stir 1¹/₂ tablespoons creamer into 8 ounces hot coffee; stir until well blended.

CHERRY-FLAVORED SUGAR

- 1¹/₂ cups sugar
- 1 package (0.13 ounce) unsweetened cherry-flavored soft drink mix

In a medium bowl, combine sugar and soft drink mix. Store in an airtight container. Give with serving instructions.

Yield: about 1¹/₂ cups flavored sugar

To serve: Stir 2 teaspoons flavored sugar into 6 ounces hot tea; stir until well blended.

CAFÉ BASKETS

For each basket, you will need a 4" x 8" clear cellophane bag, 1³/₈"w wired ribbon, hot glue gun, artificial greenery (we used holly leaves with berries), jar with lid, red and green card stock, white paper, decorative-edge craft scissors, craft glue, black permanent fine-point marker, 16¹/₂" square of fabric, natural excelsior, and a basket (we used a 7" dia. basket).

1. Place packets of coffee or tea in cellophane bag. Tie 24" of ribbon into a bow around top of bag. Hot glue a piece of greenery to knot of bow.

2. Measure around jar lid; add 6". Cut a length of ribbon the determined measurement. Knot ribbon around lid; hot glue a piece of greenery to knot of ribbon.

3. For tag, cut a 2" x 3" piece from green card stock, a 2" x 2¹/₂" piece from red card stock, and a 1⁵/₈" x 1⁷/₈" piece from white paper. Use craft scissors to trim short edges of red paper piece. Using craft glue, center and glue red card stock on green card stock and white paper on red card stock.

4. Use marker to write message on tag and draw "stitches" along edges of white paper.

5. For napkin, remove several threads from each side of fabric square to fringe edges. Place excelsior, napkin, cellophane bag, jar, and tag in basket.

HEARTWARMING LOAVES

CINNAMON-RAISIN-WALNUT BREAD

*S*hare the fresh-baked goodness of homemade bread with your neighbors. They'll appreciate the heartwarming kindness that you put into baking Cinnamon-Raisin-Walnut Bread. The recipe makes two loaves, so you can double your giving. A fabric-lined basket, topped by a cross-stitched bread cloth and tied with ribbons and bells, lends a Christmasy touch.

1 package dry yeast
1 cup warm water
4¹⁄₂ to 5 cups all-purpose flour
¹⁄₂ cup granulated sugar
³⁄₄ teaspoon salt
¹⁄₂ cup butter or margarine, melted and divided
2 eggs
1 cup raisins
Vegetable oil cooking spray
¹⁄₃ cup firmly packed brown sugar
1 tablespoon ground cinnamon
¹⁄₂ cup finely chopped walnuts
2 cups confectioners sugar
1 teaspoon vanilla extract
2¹⁄₂ tablespoons water

In a small bowl, dissolve yeast in 1 cup warm water. In a large bowl, combine 4¹⁄₂ cups flour, granulated sugar, and salt. In a small bowl, combine 6 tablespoons melted butter and eggs. Add butter mixture and yeast mixture to dry ingredients; stir until a soft dough forms. Add raisins to dough. Turn onto a lightly floured surface. Knead about 5 minutes or until dough becomes smooth and elastic and raisins are evenly distributed, using additional flour as necessary. Place in a large bowl sprayed with cooking spray, turning once to coat top of dough. Cover and let rise in a warm place (80 to 85 degrees) 1 to 1¹⁄₂ hours or until doubled in size.

In a small bowl, combine brown sugar and cinnamon. Turn dough onto a lightly floured surface and punch down. Divide dough in half. Roll each half into a 7 x 12-inch rectangle. Brush with remaining melted butter. Sprinkle each rectangle with cinnamon mixture to within 1 inch of edges. Sprinkle with walnuts. Beginning at 1 short edge, roll up each rectangle jellyroll style. Pinch seams to seal. Place loaves, seam side down, in 2 greased 4¹⁄₂ x 8¹⁄₂-inch loaf pans. Cover and let rise in a warm place 1 hour or until almost doubled in size.

Preheat oven to 350 degrees. Bake 28 to 33 minutes or until bread is golden brown. Cool in pans 10 minutes. Remove loaves from pans and cool completely on a wire rack.

In a small bowl, combine confectioners sugar, vanilla, and water; stir until smooth. Ice loaves of bread. Let icing harden. Store in an airtight container.

Yield: 2 loaves bread

CROSS-STITCHED BREAD COVER

You will need embroidery floss (see color key, page 117), 17" square White Royal Classic Bread Cover (14 ct), 20" square of red fabric, basket with side handles, 25" of 1¹⁄₄"w wired ribbon, 22mm gold jingle bell, and gold cord.

Refer to Cross Stitch, page 123, before beginning project.

1. Using three strands of floss for *Cross Stitch* and one strand of floss for *Backstitch*, stitch design, page 117, on one corner of bread cover ³⁄₄" from outer edge of fringe.
2. Use fabric and follow *Making a Basket Liner*, page 121, to make a liner with finished edges.
3. Place liner and bread cover in basket.
4. Tie ribbon into a bow around one handle of basket. Thread bell onto cord. Tie cord into a bow around handle of basket over knot of bow.

CHOCOLATE CANES

*T*raditional candy canes take on a new twist in this cheery offering. The temptingly rich Chunky Chocolate Candies are formed in cane-shaped cookie cutters, wrapped in cellophane, and embellished with curling ribbon. The recipe makes 14, so it's an ideal way for a teacher to reward students.

CHUNKY CHOCOLATE CANDIES

    3   candy bars (7 ounces each) milk
          chocolate with almonds
  $1/3$ cup flaked coconut
  $1/3$ cup miniature marshmallows
  $1/3$ cup finely chopped candied
          cherries
  $1/4$ cup raisins

In a heavy medium saucepan, melt chocolate bars over low heat. Stir in coconut, marshmallows, cherries, and raisins until well blended. Remove from heat. Spoon into fourteen $1^3/4$ x $3^1/4$-inch candy cane-shaped plastic cookie cutters that have been placed on a waxed paper-lined baking sheet. Chill 1 hour or until firm. Store in an airtight container in refrigerator.

Yield: 14 candies

COOKIE CUTTER CANDY BAGS

For each bag, you will need a 3" x 9" clear cellophane bag, two 20" lengths each of red and green curling ribbon, curling ribbon shredder, hot glue gun, 1" dia. white pom-pom, Christmas motif sticker 2" high or smaller, $2^1/2$" x 4" piece of white card stock, red and green

permanent fine-point markers, and a hole punch.

1. Place candy-filled cookie cutter in cellophane bag; knot ribbons around top of bag.
2. Curl ribbon ends. Following manufacturer's instructions, use ribbon shredder to shred streamers.

3. Glue pom-pom to knot of ribbon.
4. For tag, apply sticker to left side of card stock. Trim left side of tag along sticker shape. Use red marker to draw design along edges of tag and green marker to write message on tag. Punch hole in tag. Use a ribbon streamer to tie tag to bag.

TEACHER'S ROLL CALL

*R*ecognize a special
teacher by answering roll call
with a canister of Peppermint
Swirl Cookies! The slice-and-
bake treats, prepared from
refrigerated cookie dough and
crushed peppermint candies,
will receive top grade when
delivered in a decorated
snack can topped with a
cross-stitched sentiment.

PEPPERMINT SWIRL COOKIES

  1 package (18 ounces) refrigerated
      sugar cookie dough
 1/4 cup finely crushed peppermint
      candies (about 10 round candies)
 1/8 teaspoon red liquid food coloring

Divide sugar cookie dough in half. On
a sheet of plastic wrap, use a floured
rolling pin to roll out half of dough into
an 8-inch square. Knead peppermint
candies and food coloring into remaining
half of dough. On a separate sheet of
plastic wrap, roll out peppermint dough
into an 8-inch square. Place peppermint
dough on top of plain dough. Using
plastic wrap, roll dough into an 8-inch-
long roll. Wrap in plastic wrap and store
in refrigerator. Give with baking
instructions.

Yield: 1 roll cookie dough

To bake: Cut dough into 1/4-inch slices.
Place 2 inches apart on a lightly greased
baking sheet. Bake 8 to 10 minutes in a
350-degree oven. Cool cookies on baking
sheet 5 minutes; transfer to a wire rack to
cool completely. Store in an airtight
container.

Yield: about 2 1/2 dozen cookies

CROSS-STITCHED DOUGH CANS

For each can, you will need embroidery
floss (see color key, page 118), 5" square
of white Aida (14 ct), tracing paper,
poster board, spray adhesive, craft glue,
tall snack chip can with lid, wrapping
paper, and curling ribbon.

*Refer to Cross Stitch, page 123, before
beginning project.*

1. Using two strands of floss for *Cross
Stitch* and one strand of floss for
Backstitch, center and stitch design,
page 118, on Aida.

2. Trace around lid on tracing paper; cut
out. Using pattern, cut out design and a
circle from poster board. Apply spray
adhesive to wrong side of design. Smooth
design onto poster board circle. Glue
circle to lid; allow to dry.
3. Measure height of can; measure
around can and add 1/2". Cut a piece from
wrapping paper the determined
measurements. Apply spray adhesive to
wrong side of paper; smooth around can.
4. Tie several lengths of curling ribbon
into a bow around can; curl ends.

COFFEE BREAK

Give a co-worker a break from the holiday rush by offering this Coffee Cake Loaf. The crunchy, sweet topping is worth taking time out to savor! For a quick delivery, place a loaf in a fabric-lined basket, add a package of coffee beans and a pair of wintry mugs, and tie with raffia.

COFFEE CAKE LOAF

CAKE

- ¹/₂ cup butter or margarine, softened
- ¹/₂ cup granulated sugar
- ¹/₃ cup firmly packed brown sugar
- 1 egg
- 1¹/₂ teaspoons vanilla extract
- 1¹/₂ cups all-purpose flour
- 1 teaspoon baking powder
- ¹/₂ teaspoon baking soda
- ¹/₄ teaspoon salt
- ²/₃ cup buttermilk

TOPPING

- ¹/₄ cup firmly packed brown sugar
- 1 tablespoon butter or margarine
- ¹/₂ teaspoon ground cinnamon
- ¹/₂ cup chopped pecans

Preheat oven to 350 degrees. For cake, cream butter in a medium bowl until fluffy. Gradually beat in sugars. Add egg and vanilla; beat until well blended. In a small bowl, combine flour, baking powder, baking soda, and salt. Alternately add dry ingredients and buttermilk to creamed mixture; stir until blended.

For topping, combine brown sugar, butter, and cinnamon in a small bowl until crumbly. Stir in pecans. Spread half of batter into a greased and floured

4¹/₂ x 8¹/₂-inch loaf pan. Sprinkle with half of topping. Repeat with remaining batter and topping. Bake 50 to 55 minutes or until a toothpick inserted in center of cake comes out clean. Cover with aluminum foil if top begins to brown too quickly. Cool in pan 10 minutes. Remove from pan and serve warm or cool completely on a wire rack. Store in an airtight container.
Yield: 1 coffee cake loaf

BASKET WITH MUGS

You will need a basket (we used a 10" x 12¹/₂" basket with wire handle), fabric to line basket, natural raffia, hot

glue gun, tracing paper, yellow card stock, black permanent fine-point marker, coffee mugs, and a small bag of coffee beans.

1. For basket liner, refer to *Making a Basket Liner*, page 121, to make a liner with unfinished edges.
2. Tie several 20" lengths of raffia into a bow; glue to side of basket.
3. Trace pattern, page 118, onto tracing paper; cut out. Using pattern, cut star from card stock. Use marker to draw "stitches" along edges and write message on star. Glue star to center of bow.
4. Place fabric liner, mugs, coffee, and wrapped cake loaf in basket.

CHERRY CONFECTIONS

*S*hare some old-fashioned goodness with a neighbor and reminisce about Christmases past. Red and green chopped cherries give these chewy nougats colorful appeal. Wrap the candy in waxed paper and place in a purchased ceramic Christmas gift bag for an easy-to-create offering.

OLD-FASHIONED CANDIES

    4   cups confectioners sugar
  1/3   cup butter, softened
  1/3   cup light corn syrup
    1   teaspoon vanilla extract
  1/8   teaspoon salt
  1/2   cup chopped red candied cherries
  1/2   cup chopped green candied
          cherries
  1/2   cup chopped walnuts

Line an 8-inch square baking pan with plastic wrap, extending wrap over 2 sides of pan; set aside. In a large bowl, combine confectioners sugar, butter, corn syrup, vanilla, and salt; beat until blended. On a flat surface, knead candy until smooth and shiny (about 3 minutes). Knead in cherries and walnuts until evenly distributed. Press candy into prepared pan. Cover and chill overnight in refrigerator.

Use ends of plastic wrap to lift candy from pan. Cut into 1-inch squares. Wrap each square in waxed paper. Store in refrigerator.

Yield: about 4 dozen pieces

TWICE AS NICE

*S*hare the joy of holiday baking with our Double Chip Cookie Mix! A combination of white and chocolate chips makes the cookies twice as nice. Layer the ingredients in a jar, top with a doily, and tuck into a coordinating bag. Don't forget to include the directions!

DOUBLE CHIP COOKIE MIX

 1 cup plus 2 tablespoons all-purpose flour
 1/4 teaspoon baking powder
 1/8 teaspoon salt
 1/2 cup chopped pecans
 1/2 cup white baking chips
 1/2 cup semisweet chocolate chips
 6 tablespoons firmly packed brown sugar
 6 tablespoons granulated sugar

In a small bowl, combine flour, baking powder, and salt; stir until well blended. Spoon flour mixture into a wide-mouth 1-quart jar with lid. Layer pecans, white baking chips, chocolate chips, brown sugar, and granulated sugar in jar. Cover with lid. Give with baking instructions.

Yield: about 3 1/2 cups cookie mix

To bake: Preheat oven to 350 degrees. Pour cookie mix into a medium bowl and stir until ingredients are well blended. In a small bowl, combine 1/4 cup vegetable oil, 1 egg, 2 tablespoons milk, and 1/2 teaspoon vanilla extract; beat until blended. Add oil mixture to dry ingredients; stir until a soft dough forms. Drop rounded teaspoonfuls of dough 2 inches apart onto a greased baking sheet. Bake 8 to 10 minutes or until edges are lightly browned. Transfer to a wire rack to cool. Store in an airtight container.

Yield: about 3 dozen cookies

DOILY-WRAPPED BAG AND JAR

You will need a quart-size jar with lid, fabric, pinking shears, rubber band, two 11" dia. doilies, two 28" lengths of 3/8"w grosgrain ribbon, 6" x 11" brown paper bag, paper-backed fusible web, hole punch, and kraft paper.

1. For jar lid cover, draw around lid on wrong side of fabric. Using pinking shears, cut out circle 3" outside drawn line. Center circle over lid; secure with rubber band.

2. Place one doily over lid. Thread one ribbon length through openings in doily along lid edge. Pull ribbon ends to gather doily around lid; tie into a bow to secure.

3. For bag, cut one 6" x 11" piece each from fabric and fusible web. Fuse web to wrong side of fabric; fuse fabric to front of bag.

4. Place gift in bag. Fold top of bag 1 1/2" to back. Punch two holes 1" apart in center of folded portion of bag. Place remaining doily over top of bag. Thread remaining ribbon length through doily and holes from back to front; tie ribbon ends into a bow.

5. For tag, cut one 3" x 4 1/2" piece each from kraft paper, fabric, and fusible web. Fuse web to wrong side of fabric; fuse fabric to paper. Matching short edges, fold tag in half.

SWEET TRIO

A friend who loves sweets will scoop up this trio of Quick Dessert Sauces. All three — chocolate, marshmallow, and peppermint — start with one basic recipe, and they're all great with ice cream, cake, or other desserts. Nestle the labeled sauces in a decorative wire rack that can be used for easy serving!

QUICK DESSERT SAUCES

Make 3 separate batches of sauce for 3 different flavors.

- 1 can (14 ounces) sweetened condensed milk
- 1 cup sugar
- 2 tablespoons milk
- 1/4 cup butter
- 1 tablespoon vanilla extract

In a medium saucepan, combine sweetened condensed milk, sugar, and milk over medium heat. Stirring frequently, cook until sugar dissolves (about 12 minutes). Remove from heat. Add butter, vanilla, and ingredient(s) from one of the variations given below; stir until well blended. Serve warm. Store in an airtight container in refrigerator.

Yield: about 2 1/4 cups sauce

CHOCOLATE SAUCE: 3 squares semisweet baking chocolate

PEPPERMINT SAUCE: 1/3 cup crushed peppermint candies and 2 drops red liquid food coloring

MARSHMALLOW SAUCE: 1 cup marshmallow creme

JAR LID COVERS

For each lid cover, you will need a half-pint jar with lid, decorative tissue paper, 2mm leather lacing, thin rubber band, tracing paper, card stock, black permanent medium-point marker, and craft glue.

1. For jar lid cover, draw around lid on wrong side of tissue paper; cut out circle 1 1/4" outside drawn line. Center circle over lid; secure with rubber band. Knot a length of lacing around lid, covering rubber band.

2. For tag, trace pattern, page 118, onto tracing paper; cut out. Using pattern, cut heart from card stock. Use marker to outline edges and write message on tag. Glue tag to lid; allow to dry.

*F*ruitcake has been a Christmas tradition for generations. Now it's even easier to carry on the custom with our Easy Fruitcake Cookies. Using a package of refrigerated cookie dough, the chewy treats can be made in a snap. Place them in a Christmas-motif gift bag that you've tied with curling ribbon, and they're ready to give.

EASY FRUITCAKE COOKIES

1 package (1 pound, 2 ounces)
    refrigerated sugar cookie dough
$^{1}/_{4}$ cup all-purpose flour
$^{1}/_{2}$ teaspoon ground allspice
1 container (4 ounces) red candied
    cherries, chopped
1 container (4 ounces) green
    candied cherries, chopped
$^{1}/_{2}$ cup chopped walnuts

Let dough sit at room temperature 15 minutes. Preheat oven to 350 degrees. In a small bowl, combine flour and allspice. Break up dough in a large bowl. Sprinkle flour mixture over dough; stir until flour is incorporated. Stir in cherries and walnuts. Drop teaspoonfuls of dough 2 inches apart onto a greased baking sheet. Bake 9 to 11 minutes or until edges are lightly browned. Transfer cookies to a wire rack to cool. Store in an airtight container.

Yield: about $4^{1}/_{2}$ dozen cookies

"MERRY CHRISTMAS" BAGS

For each bag, you will need a lunch-size Christmas-motif gift bag, hole punch, two 21" lengths of gold cord, assorted colors of curling ribbon, tracing paper, gold card stock, black permanent fine-point marker, and a hot glue gun.

1. Place cookies in bag. Fold top of bag 1$^{1}/_{2}$" to back. At each side of bag, punch a hole in folded portion of bag. Thread one length of cord and several lengths of ribbon through hole; tie into a bow. Curl ribbon ends.
2. For tag, trace pattern, page 119, onto tracing paper; cut out. Using pattern, cut star from card stock. Use marker to write message on tag. Glue tag to bag.

STAR ATTRACTION

*T*his Lemon Chess Pie will be the star attraction at your office Christmas party. A flavorful combination of traditional chess and pecan pies, this dessert is highlighted by a constellation of pastry cutouts. A napkin-lined basket makes a handy carrier.

LEMON CHESS PIE

CRUST

- 1¼ cups all-purpose flour
- ½ teaspoon salt
- ⅓ cup vegetable shortening
- 3 to 4 tablespoons cold water

FILLING

- ½ cup butter or margarine, softened
- 2 cups sugar
- 1 tablespoon all-purpose flour
- 1 tablespoon white cornmeal
- 5 eggs
- ¾ cup milk
- 2 tablespoons freshly squeezed lemon juice
- 1 teaspoon vanilla extract
- ½ teaspoon lemon extract
- 1½ cups chopped pecans

For crust, combine flour and salt in a medium bowl. Using a pastry blender or 2 knives, cut in shortening until mixture resembles coarse meal. Sprinkle with cold water. Mix until a soft dough forms. On a lightly floured surface, roll out dough to a 13-inch circle. Transfer to a deep-dish 10-inch pie plate. Trim edge of dough and crimp with a fork; set aside. Reserve dough scraps for decoration.

Preheat oven to 400 degrees. For filling, cream butter and sugar in a large bowl. Beat in flour, cornmeal, eggs, milk, lemon juice, and extracts until well blended. Stir in pecans. Pour mixture into prepared crust. Roll out reserved dough to ⅛-inch thickness. Using a 1½-inch star-shaped cookie cutter, cut out stars and press lightly onto edge of pie crust. Bake pie 10 minutes. Reduce heat to 350 degrees and bake 35 to 40 minutes or until center is set. If crust browns too quickly, cover with a strip of aluminum foil. Cool and store in an airtight container in refrigerator.

Yield: about 8 servings

BASKET WITH NAPKIN LINER

You will need four ½" dia. cabone rings, 17" square fabric napkin, 10" square basket, 12" of ⅛"w satin ribbon, tracing paper, green card stock, gold paint pen, black permanent fine-point marker, and a hole punch.

1. Sew one ring to each corner of napkin.
2. Line basket with napkin. Place pie in basket.
3. Fold napkin over pie. Thread ribbon through rings and tie into a bow.
4. For tag, trace pattern, page 119, onto tracing paper; cut out. Using pattern, cut tag from card stock. Use paint pen and marker to add details and write message on tag. Punch hole in tag. Attach tag to streamer of bow.

COUNTDOWN JELLY

*O*ur *Cranberry-Champagne Jelly will give new meaning to New Year's "toasts!" Champagne left over from holiday celebrations combines with cranberry juice cocktail and orange juice to make this fruity spread. The clock-face jar topper signals that it's time to enjoy!*

CRANBERRY-CHAMPAGNE JELLY

Flat champagne works best — a great use for leftover champagne.

      3 cups cranberry juice cocktail
    1/4 cup orange juice
      1 tablespoon grated orange zest
      1 package (1 3/4 ounces) powdered
            fruit pectin
      4 cups sugar
   1 1/4 cups flat champagne

In a Dutch oven, combine cranberry juice, orange juice, orange zest, and pectin over medium-high heat. Bring to a rolling boil. Add sugar. Stirring constantly, bring to a rolling boil again and boil 1 minute. Remove from heat; stir in champagne. Skim off foam. Spoon jelly into heat-resistant jars; cover and cool to room temperature. Store in refrigerator.

Yield: about 6 cups jelly

NEW YEAR'S JAR

You will need colored pencils, photocopy of clock pattern (page 120) on white card stock, half-pint wide-mouth canning jar with lid and band, craft glue, 24" of 7/8"w red wired ribbon, shredded Mylar™, black felt top hat with 3" dia. opening,

gold and black permanent fine-point markers, 1 3/8" x 2 3/4" piece of white card stock for tag, 3" of 1 5/8"w gold mesh ribbon, hole punch, and gold cord.

1. Use pencils to color photocopy. Center opening of jar band over clock. Draw around outside of band; cut out.
2. Place lid on jar; glue clock to lid. Twist band onto jar.

3. Matching long edges, fold wired ribbon in half lengthwise. Tie into a bow around band.
4. Place Mylar and jar in hat.
5. Use gold and black markers to write message on tag. Center and glue tag on mesh ribbon; allow to dry. Punch hole in corner of tag. Thread cord through hole and knot ends together.

LAYERS OF FLAVOR

Offer a special couple on your list this delightful appetizer basket. Our cheese spread is layered with flavor, as well as visual appeal. Include a jar of the spread, crackers, and Christmas goblets for a "vintage" gift.

WINE-TIME CHEESE SPREAD

    1 package (8 ounces) cream cheese,
          softened
    2 cups (8 ounces) shredded sharp
          Cheddar cheese
  ½ cup sour cream
    1 teaspoon dried Italian seasoning
  ½ teaspoon hot pepper sauce
    4 ounces Genoa salami, finely
          chopped
    1 jar (5 ounces) pimiento-stuffed
          green olives, drained and finely
          chopped
       Crackers to serve

In a medium bowl, beat cream cheese until fluffy. Add Cheddar cheese, sour cream, Italian seasoning, and pepper sauce; beat until well blended. Layer salami and olives between layers of cheese mixture in 2 pint-size jars. Cover and chill 24 hours to let flavors blend. Serve with crackers.

Yield: about 4 cups cheese spread

WINE GOBLET BASKET

You will need 30" of 1½"w wired ribbon, 4" dia. airtight jar with knobbed lid, artificial greenery (we used a sprig of holly leaves with berries), oval basket (we used a 10" x 14" oval basket), white shredded paper, and two decorative goblets.

1. Tie ribbon into a bow around knob on jar lid. Insert ends of greenery under knot of bow.
2. Line basket with shredded paper. Arrange goblets, a bag of crackers, and gift jar in basket.

WINTER WONDERLAND CAKE

To: the Clarks
From: the Sims

A winter wonderland of flavor, our Pineapple-Macadamia Cake is an elegant addition to any holiday table. Pineapple preserves and chopped macadamia nuts are at the heart of the cake, which is crowned with snowy cream cheese-coconut frosting.

PINEAPPLE-MACADAMIA CAKE

CAKE

- 1 cup butter or margarine, softened
- 1½ cups sugar
- 1 teaspoon vanilla extract
- 4 eggs
- 3 cups sifted cake flour
- 1 teaspoon baking soda
- ¼ teaspoon salt
- ¾ cup buttermilk
- 1 jar (12 ounces) pineapple preserves
- 1 cup chopped macadamia nuts

ICING

- 1 package (8 ounces) cream cheese, softened
- ¼ cup butter or margarine, softened
- 1 teaspoon vanilla extract
- 1 package (16 ounces) confectioners sugar
- 1 cup flaked coconut
- 1 jar (12 ounces) pineapple preserves

Preheat oven to 350 degrees. For cake, grease three 9-inch round cake pans. Line bottoms with waxed paper; grease waxed paper. In a large bowl, cream butter, sugar, and vanilla until fluffy. Add eggs, 1 at a time, beating well after each addition. In a medium bowl, combine cake flour, baking soda, and salt. Alternately beat dry ingredients and buttermilk into creamed mixture, beating until well blended. Stir in preserves and macadamia nuts. Spoon batter into prepared pans. Bake 25 to 30 minutes or until a toothpick inserted in center of cake comes out clean. Cool in pans 5 minutes. Remove from pans and cool completely on a wire rack.

For icing, beat cream cheese, butter, and vanilla in a medium bowl until fluffy. Add confectioners sugar; beat until smooth. Stir in coconut. To assemble cake, place 1 cake layer on a serving plate. Spread half of preserves over top of layer. Place second cake layer on top of first. Spread remaining preserves over top of layer. Place remaining cake layer on top. Spread icing on top and sides of cake. Store in an airtight container in refrigerator.

Yield: about 16 servings

COVERED CAKE BOX

You will need a 10" square x 5½"h cake box, wrapping paper, spray adhesive, craft knife, cutting mat, one 2⅔ yds. length and one 1⅓ yds. length of 2½"w wired ribbon, 6" of floral wire, decorative-edge craft scissors, white and red card stock, Christmas sticker, hole punch, black permanent fine-point marker, and 12" of ¼"w satin ribbon.

1. Unfold box. Cut a piece from wrapping paper 1" larger on all sides than box. Place wrapping paper wrong side up on a flat surface. Apply spray adhesive to outside of box. Center box adhesive side down on paper; press firmly to secure.
2. Use craft knife to cut paper even with edges of box. If box has slits, use craft knife to cut through slits from inside of box. Reassemble box.
3. Place cake in box.
4. Beginning with center of 2⅔ yds. ribbon across top of box, wrap ribbon to bottom, twist ribbon, and bring ends to top of box; tie ends into a bow. Using remaining wired ribbon, follow *Making a Bow*, page 121, to make a bow with six 7" loops and two 3" streamers. Use wire to attach bow to knot of first bow.
5. For tag, use craft scissors to cut a 1¾" x 2¾" piece from white card stock. Apply spray adhesive to one side of tag and smooth onto red card stock. Leaving a ¼" red border, use craft scissors to cut out tag. Apply sticker to one corner of tag; punch hole in opposite corner. Use marker to write message on tag. Use satin ribbon to attach tag to bow.

PATTERNS

SNOWMAN CROSS STITCH MUG

(page 17)

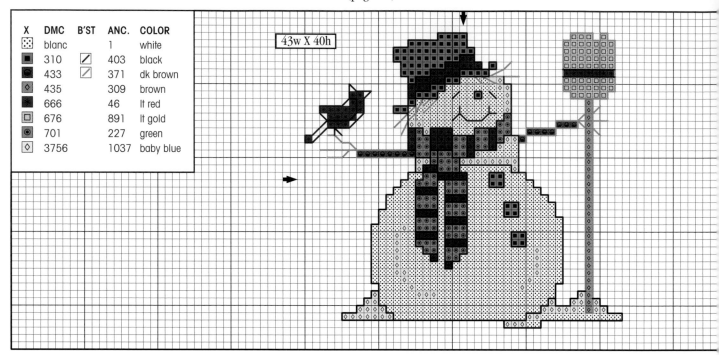

X	DMC	B'ST	ANC.	COLOR
⬚	blanc		1	white
◼	310	╱	403	black
◼	433	╱	371	dk brown
◈	435		309	brown
✳	666		46	lt red
▢	676		891	lt gold
⊙	701		227	green
◇	3756		1037	baby blue

43w X 40h

STAR RIBBON BASKET

(page 18)

TREE TOTE BAG

(page 21)

CROSS-STITCHED TAGS

(page 74)

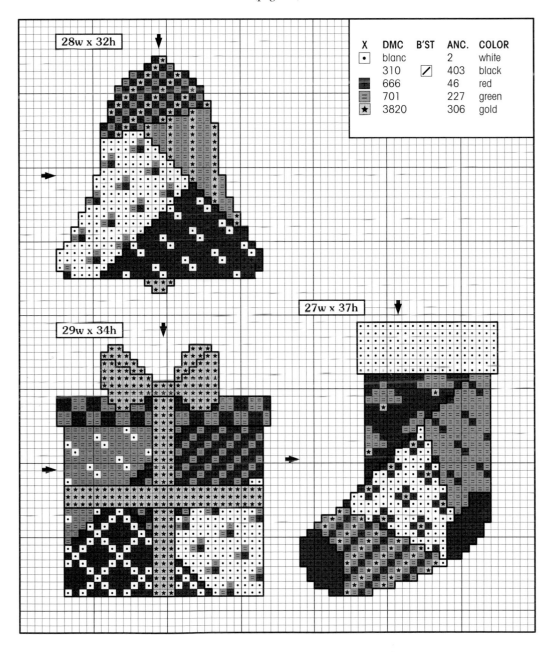

X	DMC	B'ST	ANC.	COLOR
•	blanc		2	white
	310	∕	403	black
	666		46	red
−	701		227	green
★	3820		306	gold

28w x 32h

29w x 34h

27w x 37h

"NOEL" BAG AND JAR LID COVER

(page 26)

*Leisure Arts, Inc., grants permission to the owner
of this book to photocopy the design on this page
for personal use only.*

GRANOLA WRAPPERS

(page 42)

Leisure Arts, Inc., grants permission to the owner of this book to photocopy the "Granola Wrapper" design on this page for personal use only.

HOT PEPPER SLEEVES

(page 27)

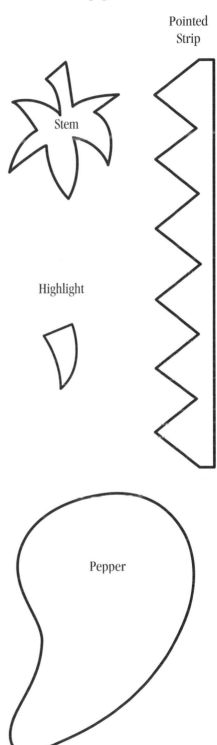

Pointed Strip

Stem

Highlight

Pepper

SANTA CROSS STITCH BOX

(page 30)

X	DMC	¼X	B'ST
⊡	blanc	⊡	
▨	304		
■	310		◪
V	317		
■	321		
⊡	415		
◆	433		
★	435		
△	436		
—	437		
◻	666		
◐	699		
+	725		
◉	754		
○	760		
✕	762		
◆	782		
◎	783	◪	◪
◇ ★	910 & 009		
▢ ★	911 & 009		
▢ ★	912 & 009		
▢	948		
▨	3799		
●	310	black french knot	
●	498	dk red french knot	

★ Use 5 strands of floss and 2 strands of Kreinik
Blending Filament #009HL emerald

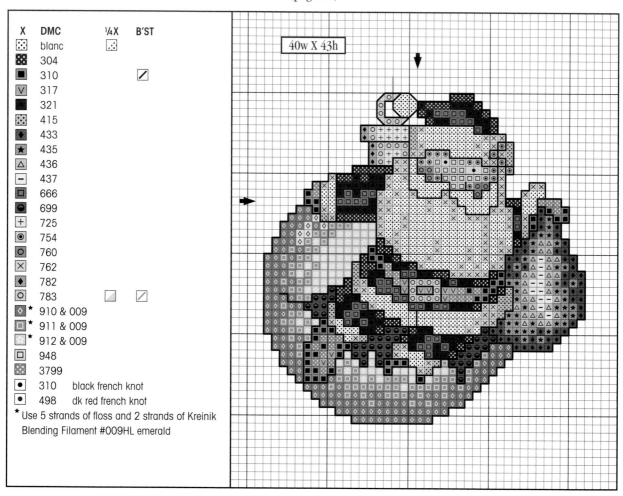

40w X 43h

SNOWMAN BASKET
(page 32)

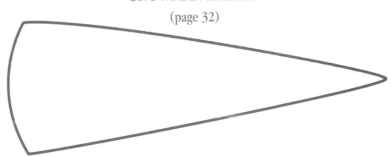

ROUND ORNAMENT COOKIES
(page 31)

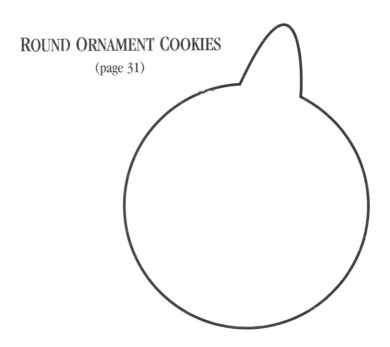

STIR-FRY SAUCE LABEL
(page 37)

STIR-
FRY
SAUCE

"NOEL" POT HOLDER
(page 33)

PATTERNS (continued)

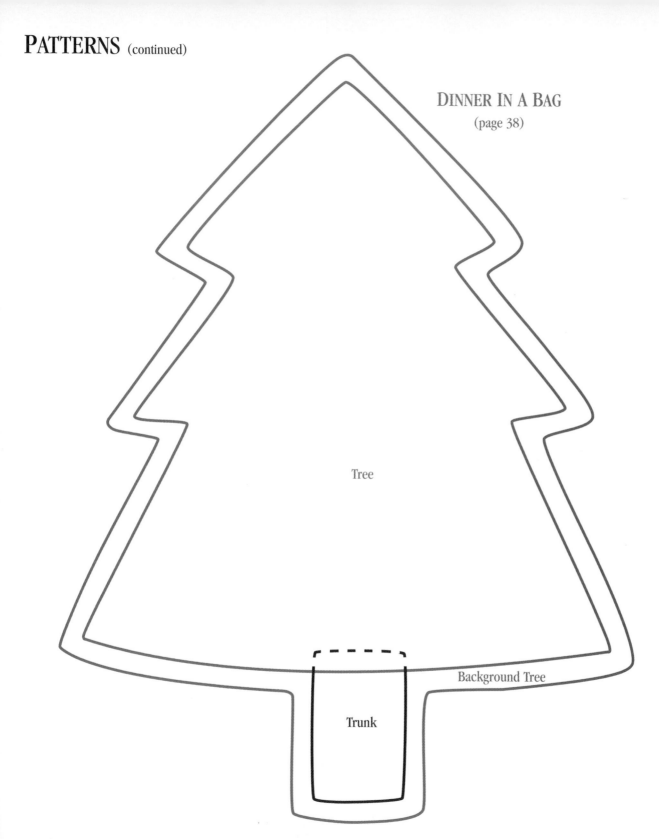

DINNER IN A BAG
(page 38)

Tree

Background Tree

Trunk

JAR LID TOPPER AND TAG
(page 50)

GREEN STAR CANDY BOX
(page 44)

APPLIQUÉD TOWEL BAG
(page 41)

HOBBY NUT GIFT BAGS
(page 53)

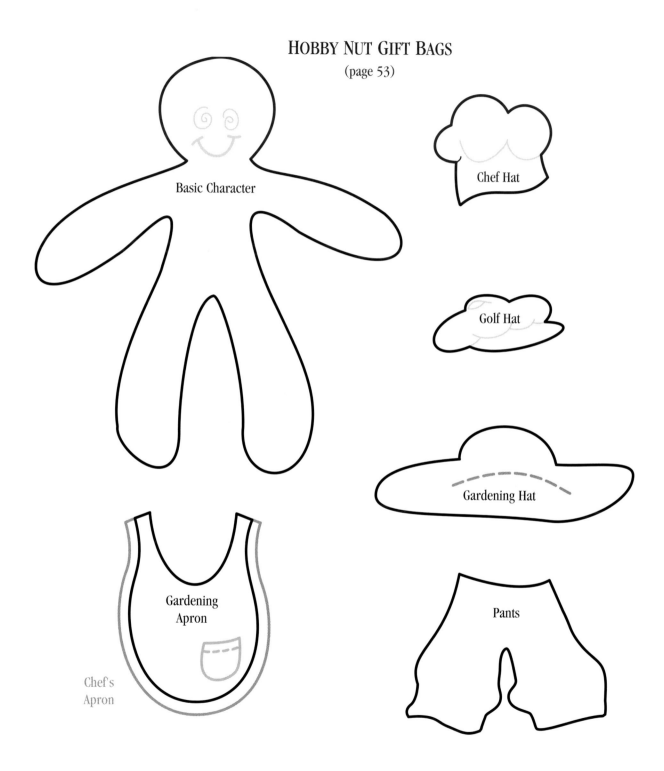

Basic Character

Chef Hat

Golf Hat

Gardening Hat

Gardening Apron

Chef's Apron

Pants

SANTA JAR WITH HAT

(page 54)

PATTERNS (continued)

SNOWMAN CANVAS BAG
(page 55)

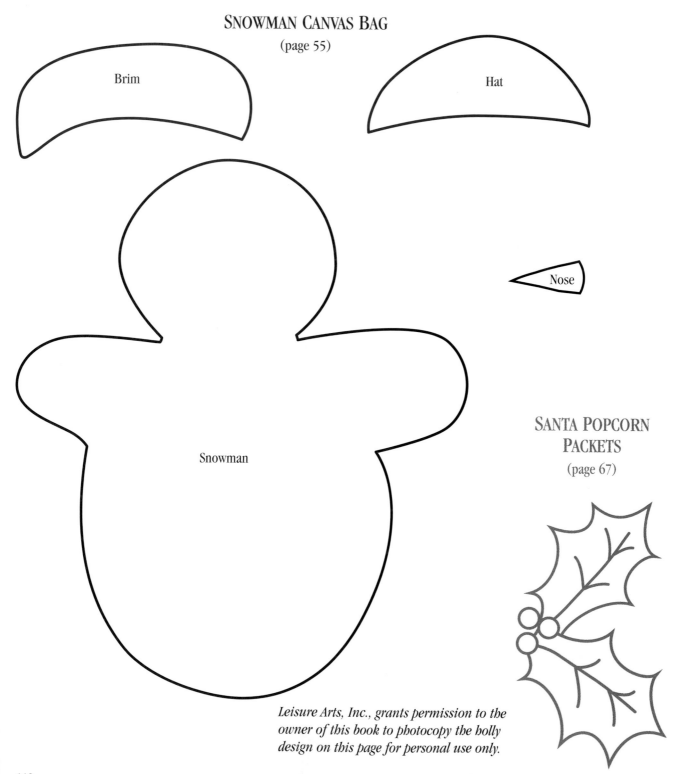

Brim

Hat

Nose

Snowman

SANTA POPCORN PACKETS
(page 67)

Leisure Arts, Inc., grants permission to the owner of this book to photocopy the holly design on this page for personal use only.

JAR WITH CROSS STITCH ORNAMENT

(page 57)

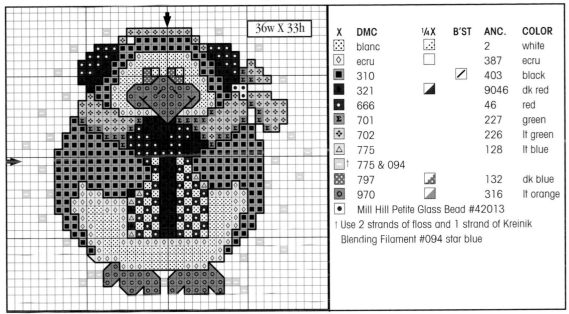

36w X 33h

X	DMC	¼X	B'ST	ANC.	COLOR
⊡	blanc	⊡		2	white
◇	ecru	☐		387	ecru
■	310		╱	403	black
◼	321		◣	9046	dk red
◼	666			46	red
Σ	701			227	green
✷	702			226	lt green
△	775			128	lt blue
☐†	775 & 094				
⊠	797		◪	132	dk blue
⊙	970		◿	316	lt orange
●	Mill Hill Petite Glass Bead #42013				

† Use 2 strands of floss and 1 strand of Kreinik
Blending Filament #094 star blue

SANTA POPCORN PACKETS

(page 67)

Leisure Arts, Inc., grants permission to the owner of this book to photocopy the label on this page for personal use only.

Just Poppin' in to say Merry Christmas!

PATTERNS (continued)

Head

Wings

ANGEL BOX
(page 69)

Body

Small Star

Tree

Large Star

BAGEL SPREAD PACKETS
(page 70)

Leisure Arts, Inc., grants permission to the owner of this book to photocopy the label design on this page for personal use only.

To serve: Process 2 teaspoons mix with one 8-ounce package softened cream cheese in a food processor until smooth. Transfer to an airtight container. Chill 2 hours to let flavors blend. Serve spread on bagel slices.

HOLIDAY BASKET ENSEMBLE
(page 71)

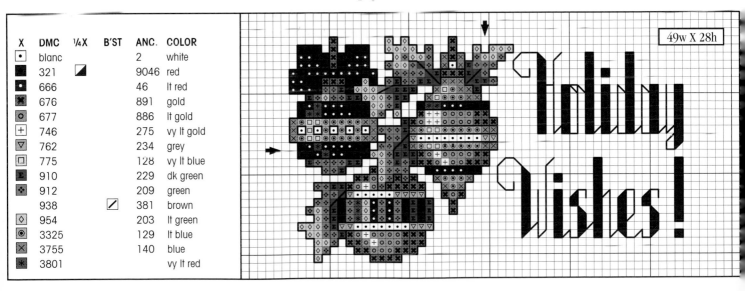

X	DMC	¼X	B'ST	ANC.	COLOR
•	blanc			2	white
■	321	◹		9046	red
▨	666			46	lt red
✹	676			891	gold
◉	677			886	lt gold
＋	746			275	vy lt gold
▽	762			234	grey
▢	775			128	vy lt blue
⊠	910			229	dk green
❖	912			209	green
	938		◿	381	brown
◇	954			203	lt green
◉	3325			129	lt blue
✕	3755			140	blue
✳	3801				vy lt red

49w X 28h

115

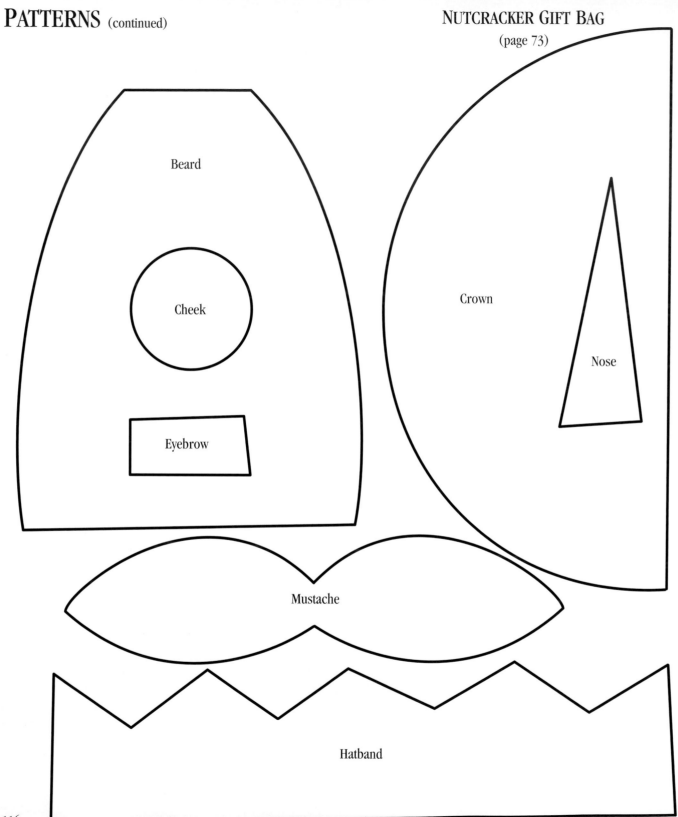

Beard

Crown

Cheek

Nose

Eyebrow

Mustache

Hatband

CROSS-STITCHED BREAD COVER

(page 89)

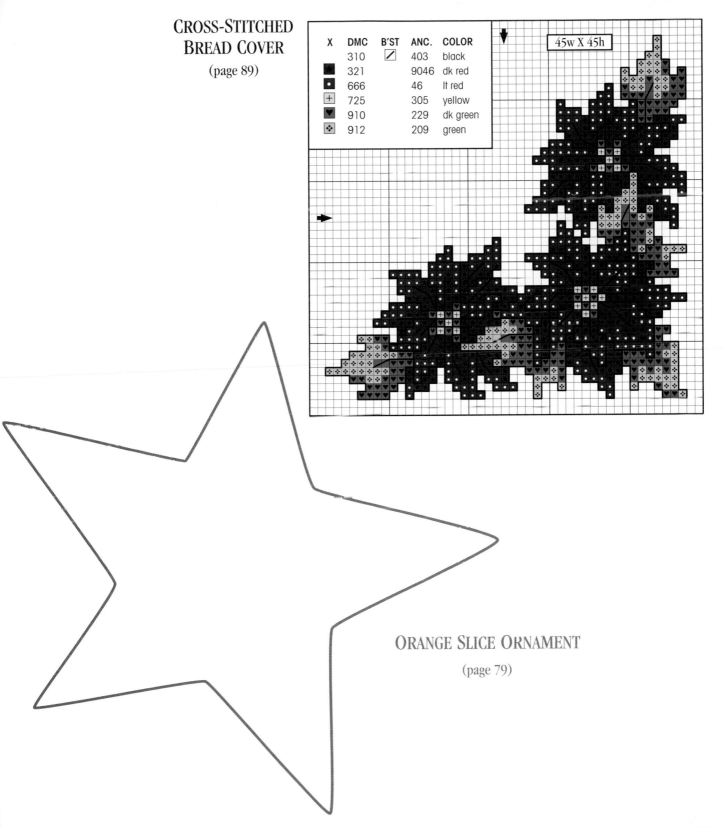

X	DMC	B'ST	ANC.	COLOR
	310	╱	403	black
	321		9046	dk red
	666		46	lt red
+	725		305	yellow
	910		229	dk green
	912		209	green

45w X 45h

ORANGE SLICE ORNAMENT

(page 79)

PATTERNS (continued)

CROSS-STITCHED DOUGH CANS
(page 91)

X	DMC	B'ST	ANC.	COLOR
⬚	blanc		2	white
⬛	498		1005	dk maroon
✳	552	╱	99	dk purple
⬛	666	╱	46	red
▲	699	╱	923	emerald green
⊙	744		301	lt yellow
☆	775		300	lt sky blue
✳	838	╱	380	vy dk beige brown
•	699			emerald green French Knot

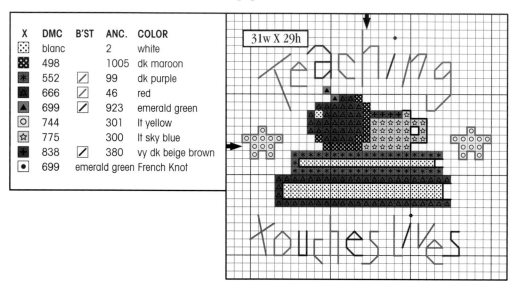

31w X 29h

BASKET WITH MUGS
(page 92)

JAR LID COVERS
(page 95)

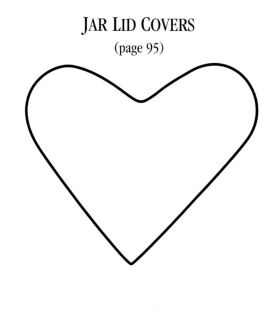

"MERRY CHRISTMAS" BAGS
(page 96)

BASKET WITH NAPKIN LINER
(page 97)

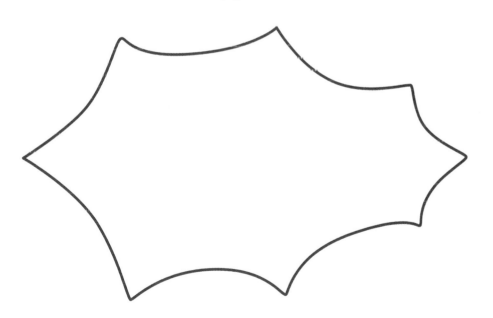

PATTERNS (continued)

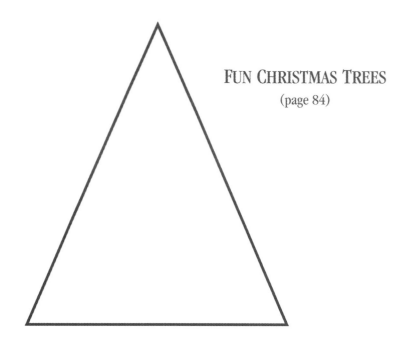

FUN CHRISTMAS TREES
(page 84)

NEW YEAR'S JAR
(page 98)

Leisure Arts, Inc., grants permission to the owner of this book to photocopy the clock pattern design on this page for personal use only.

GENERAL INSTRUCTIONS

ABOUT THE PAPER WE USED

For many of the projects in this book, we used white and colored paper. There are a variety of papers for these projects available at copy centers or craft stores. When selecting paper, choose one that is suitable in weight for the project. We used copier paper, card and cover stock, construction paper, poster board, bristol board, and handmade paper.

ABOUT ADHESIVES

Refer to the following list when selecting adhesives. Carefully follow the manufacturer's instructions when applying adhesives.

CRAFT GLUE: Recommended for paper, fabric, wood, and floral items. Dry flat or secure with clothespins or straight pins until glue is dry.

FABRIC GLUE: Recommended for fabric or paper items. Dry flat or secure with clothespins or straight pins until glue is dry.

HOT/LOW-TEMPERATURE GLUE GUN AND GLUE STICKS: Recommended for paper, fabric, and floral items; hold in place until set. Dries quickly. Low-temperature glue does not hold as well as hot glue, but offers a safer gluing option.

CRAFT GLUE STICK: Recommended for small, lightweight items. Dry flat.

SPRAY ADHESIVE: Recommended for adhering paper or fabric items. Dry flat.

RUBBER CEMENT: Recommended for adhering paper to paper; dries quickly.

DECOUPAGE GLUE: Recommended for applying fabric or paper pieces to smooth surfaces.

HOUSEHOLD CEMENT: Used for ceramic and metal items; secure until set.

MAKING A BASKET LINER

For liner with an unfinished edge, cut or tear a fabric piece 1/4" larger on all sides than desired finished size of liner. Fringe edges of fabric piece 1/4" or use pinking shears to trim edges.

For liner with a finished edge, cut a fabric piece 1/2" larger on all sides than desired finished size of liner. Press edges of fabric piece 1/4" to wrong side; press 1/4" to wrong side again and stitch in place.

MAKING A BOW

Loop sizes given in project instructions refer to the length of ribbon used to make one loop of bow.

1. For first streamer, measure desired length of streamer from one end of ribbon; twist ribbon between fingers (Fig. 1).

Fig. 1

2. Keeping right side of ribbon facing out, fold ribbon to front to form desired-size loop; gather ribbon between fingers (Fig. 2). Fold ribbon to back to form another loop; gather ribbon between fingers (Fig. 3).

Fig. 2

Fig. 3

3. If a center loop is desired, form half the desired number of loops, then loosely wrap ribbon around thumb and gather ribbon between fingers (Fig. 4). Continue to form loops, varying size of loops as desired, until bow is desired size.

Fig. 4

4. For remaining streamer, trim ribbon to desired length.

5. To secure bow, hold gathered loops tightly. Fold a length of floral wire around gathers of loops. Hold wire ends behind bow, gathering all loops forward; twist bow to tighten wire. Arrange loops and trim ribbon ends as desired.

MAKING APPLIQUÉS

Follow all steps for each appliqué. When tracing patterns for more than one appliqué, leave at least 1" between shapes on web.

To make a reverse appliqué, trace pattern onto tracing paper, turn traced pattern over, and follow all steps using traced pattern.

Continued on page 122

When an appliqué pattern contains shaded areas, trace along entire outer line for appliqué indicated in project instructions. Trace outer lines of shaded areas for additional appliqués indicated in project instructions.

1. Trace appliqué pattern onto paper side of web. (Some pieces may be given as measurements. Draw shape the measurements given in project instructions on paper side of web.) Cutting about 1/2" outside drawn lines, cut out web shape.

2. Follow manufacturer's instructions to fuse web shape to wrong side of fabric. Cut out shape along drawn lines.

MAKING PATTERNS

When entire pattern is shown, place tracing paper over pattern and trace pattern; cut out. For a more durable pattern, use a permanent pen to trace pattern onto stencil plastic; cut out.

When only half of pattern is shown (indicated by blue line on pattern), fold tracing paper in half and place fold along blue line of pattern. Trace pattern half; turn folded paper over and draw over traced lines on remaining side of paper. Unfold paper and cut out pattern. For a more durable pattern, use a permanent pen to trace pattern half onto stencil plastic; turn stencil plastic over and align blue line with traced pattern half to form a whole pattern. Trace pattern half again; cut out.

When patterns are stacked or overlapped, place tracing paper over pattern and follow a single colored line to trace pattern. Repeat to trace each pattern separately onto tracing paper.

PAINTING TECHNIQUES

TRANSFERRING A PATTERN
Trace pattern onto tracing paper. Using removable tape, tape pattern to project. Place transfer paper coated side down between project and tracing paper. Use a stylus or an old ball point pen that does not write to transfer outlines of basecoat areas of design to project (press lightly to avoid smudges and heavy lines that are difficult to cover). If necessary, use a soft eraser to remove any smudges.

PAINTING BASECOATS
A disposable foam plate makes a good palette.

Use a medium round brush for large areas and a small round brush for small areas. Do not overload brush. Allowing to dry between coats, apply several thin coats of paint to project.

TRANSFERRING DETAILS
To transfer detail lines to design, replace pattern and transfer paper over painted basecoats and use stylus to lightly transfer detail lines onto project.

ADDING DETAILS
Use a permanent marker to draw over detail lines.

SPATTER PAINTING
Cover work area with paper and wear old clothes when spatter painting. Before painting item, practice painting technique on scrap paper.

1. Place item on flat surface.
2. Mix one part paint to one part water. Dip toothbrush in diluted paint and pull thumb firmly across bristles to spatter paint on item. Repeat until desired effect is achieved. Allow to dry.

SPONGE PAINTING
Use an assembly-line method when making several sponge-painted projects. Place project on a covered work surface. Practice sponge-painting technique on scrap paper until desired look is achieved. Paint projects with first color and allow to dry before moving to next color. Use a clean sponge for each additional color.

For allover designs, dip a dampened sponge piece into paint; remove excess paint on a paper towel. Use a light stamping motion to paint item.

For painting with sponge shapes, dip a dampened sponge shape into paint; remove excess paint on a paper towel. Lightly press sponge shape onto project. Carefully lift sponge. For a reverse design, turn sponge shape over.

JAR LID FINISHING

1. For jar lid insert, use flat part of a jar lid (same size as jar lid used in storing food) as a pattern and cut out one circle each from cardboard, batting, and fabric. Use craft glue to glue batting circle to cardboard circle. Center fabric circle right side up on batting; glue edges of fabric circle to batting. Allow to dry.

2. Just before presenting gift, remove band from filled jar; place jar lid insert in band and replace band over lid.

CROSS STITCH

CROSS STITCH (X)

Work one Cross Stitch to correspond to each colored square in chart. For horizontal rows, work stitches in two journeys (Fig. 1). For vertical rows, complete each stitch as shown in Fig. 2.

Fig. 1

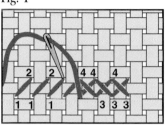

Fig. 2

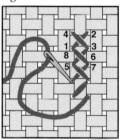

BACKSTITCH (B'ST)

For outline detail, Backstitch (shown in chart and color key by black or colored straight lines) should be worked after design has been completed (Fig. 3).

Fig. 3

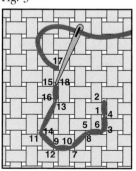

EMBROIDERY STITCHES

CROSS STITCH

Bring needle up at 1 and go down at 2. Come up at 3 and go down at 4 (Fig. 1).

Fig. 1

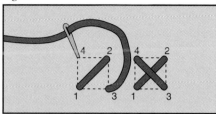

FRENCH KNOT

Bring needle up at 1. Wrap thread once around needle and insert needle at 2, holding thread with non-stitching fingers (Fig. 2). Tighten knot as close to fabric as possible while pulling needle back through fabric.

Fig. 2

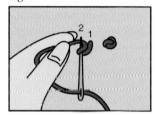

RUNNING STITCH

Make a series of straight stitches with stitch length equal to the space between stitches (Fig. 3).

Fig. 3

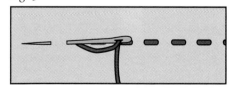

STEM STITCH

Bring needle up at 1; keeping thread below the stitching line, go down at 2 and bring needle up at 3. Take needle down at 4 and bring needle up at 5 (Fig. 4).

Fig. 4

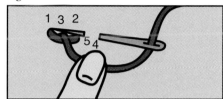

STRAIGHT STITCH

Bring needle up at 1 and go down at 2 (Fig. 5). Length of stitches may be varied as desired.

Fig. 5

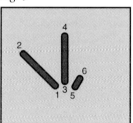

KITCHEN TIPS

MEASURING INGREDIENTS

Liquid measuring cups have a rim above the measuring line to keep liquid ingredients from spilling. Nested measuring cups are used to measure dry ingredients, butter, shortening, and peanut butter. Measuring spoons are used for measuring both dry and liquid ingredients.

To measure flour or granulated sugar: Spoon ingredient into nested measuring cup and level off with a knife. Do not pack down with spoon.

To measure confectioners sugar: Lightly spoon sugar into nested measuring cup and level off with a knife.

To measure brown sugar: Pack sugar into nested measuring cup and level off with a knife. Sugar should hold its shape when removed from cup.

To measure dry ingredients equaling less than 1/4 cup: Dip measuring spoon into ingredient and level off with a knife.

To measure butter, shortening, or peanut butter: Pack ingredient firmly into nested measuring cup and level off with a knife.

To measure liquids: Use a liquid measuring cup placed on a flat surface. Pour ingredient into cup and check measuring line at eye level.

To measure honey or syrup: For a more accurate measurement, lightly spray measuring cup or spoon with vegetable oil cooking spray before measuring so the liquid will release easily from cup or spoon.

TESTS FOR CANDY MAKING

To determine the correct temperature of cooked candy, use a candy thermometer and the cold water test. Before each use, check the accuracy of your candy thermometer by attaching it to the side of a small saucepan of water, making sure thermometer does not touch bottom of pan. Bring water to a boil. Thermometer should register 212 degrees in boiling water. If it does not, adjust the temperature range for each candy consistency accordingly.

When using a candy thermometer, insert thermometer into candy mixture, making sure thermometer does not touch bottom of pan. Read temperature at eye level. Cook candy to desired temperature range. Working quickly, drop about 1/2 teaspoon of candy mixture into a cup of ice water. Use a fresh cup of water for each test. Use the following descriptions to determine if candy has reached the correct stage:

Soft-Ball Stage (234 to 240 degrees): Candy can be rolled into a soft ball in ice water but will flatten when removed from water.

Firm-Ball Stage (242 to 248 degrees): Candy can be rolled into a firm ball in ice water but will flatten if pressed when removed from water.

Hard-Ball Stage (250 to 268 degrees): Candy can be rolled into a hard ball in ice water and will remain hard when removed from water.

Soft-Crack Stage (270 to 290 degrees): Candy will form hard threads in ice water but will soften when removed from water.

Hard-Crack Stage (300 to 310 degrees): Candy will form brittle threads in ice water and will remain brittle when removed from water.

SOFTENING BUTTER OR MARGARINE

To soften 1 stick of butter, remove wrapper and place butter on a microwave-safe plate. Microwave on medium-low power (30%) 20 to 30 seconds.

SOFTENING CREAM CHEESE

To soften cream cheese, remove wrapper and place cream cheese on a microwave-safe plate. Microwave on medium power (50%) 1 to 1 1/2 minutes for an 8-ounce package or 30 to 45 seconds for a 3-ounce package.

SHREDDING CHEESE

To shred cheese easily, place wrapped cheese in freezer 10 to 20 minutes before shredding.

TOASTING NUTS

To toast nuts, spread nuts on an ungreased baking sheet. Stirring occasionally, bake in a 350-degree oven 5 to 8 minutes or until nuts are slightly darker in color.

PREPARING CITRUS FRUIT ZEST

To remove the zest (colored outer portion of peel) from citrus fruits, use a fine grater or citrus zester, being careful not to grate bitter white portion of peel.

TOASTING COCONUT

To toast coconut, spread a thin layer of coconut on an ungreased baking sheet. Stirring occasionally, bake in a 350-degree oven 5 to 7 minutes or until coconut is lightly browned.

WHIPPING CREAM

For greatest volume, chill a glass bowl and beaters before beating whipping cream. In warm weather, place chilled bowl over ice while beating whipping cream.

SUBSTITUTING HERBS

To substitute fresh herbs for dried, use 1 tablespoon fresh chopped herbs for 1/2 teaspoon dried herbs.

CUTTING OUT COOKIES

Place a piece of white paper or stencil plastic over pattern. Use a permanent felt-tip pen with fine point to trace pattern; cut out pattern. Place pattern on rolled-out dough and use a small sharp knife to cut out cookies. (*Note:* If dough is sticky, frequently dip knife into flour while cutting out cookies.)

MELTING CHOCOLATE

To melt chocolate, place chopped or shaved chocolate in top of a double boiler over hot, not simmering, water. Using a dry spoon, stir occasionally until chocolate melts. Remove from heat and use as desired. If necessary, chocolate may be returned to heat to remelt.

EQUIVALENT MEASUREMENTS

1 tablespoon	=	3 teaspoons
1/8 cup (1 fluid ounce)	=	2 tablespoons
1/4 cup (2 fluid ounces)	=	4 tablespoons
1/3 cup	=	5 1/3 tablespoons
1/2 cup (4 fluid ounces)	=	8 tablespoons
3/4 cup (6 fluid ounces)	=	12 tablespoons
1 cup (8 fluid ounces)	=	16 tablespoons or 1/2 pint
2 cups (16 fluid ounces)	=	1 pint
1 quart (32 fluid ounces)	=	2 pints
1/2 gallon (64 fluid ounces)	=	2 quarts
1 gallon (128 fluid ounces)	=	4 quarts

HELPFUL FOOD EQUIVALENTS

1/2 cup butter	=	1 stick butter
1 square baking chocolate	=	1 ounce chocolate
1 cup chocolate chips	=	6 ounces chocolate chips
2 1/4 cups packed brown sugar	=	1 pound brown sugar
3 1/2 cups unsifted confectioners sugar	=	1 pound confectioners sugar
2 cups granulated sugar	=	1 pound granulated sugar
4 cups all-purpose flour	=	1 pound all-purpose flour
1 cup shredded cheese	=	4 ounces cheese
3 cups sliced carrots	=	1 pound carrots
1/2 cup chopped celery	=	1 rib celery
1/2 cup chopped onion	=	1 medium onion
1 cup chopped green pepper	=	1 large green pepper

RECIPE INDEX

CREDITS

To Magna IV Color Imaging of Little Rock, Arkansas, we say *thank you* for the superb color reproduction and excellent pre-press preparation.

We want to especially thank photographers Mark Mathews, Ken West, and Larry Pennington of Peerless Photography, Little Rock, Arkansas, for their time, patience, and excellent work.

To the talented people who helped in the creation of the following recipes and projects in this book, we extend a special word of thanks:

- *Snowman Cross Stitch Mug* design, page 17: Linda Gillum and Barbara Baatz
- *Homer's Award-Winning Fruitcake*, page 25: Homer Rogers
- *Button Basket*, page 29: Holly Witt
- *Santa Cross Stitch Box* design, page 30: Vicky Howard
- *Cross Stitch Ornament* design, page 57: Terrie Lee Steinmeyer
- *Vegetable Casserole*, page 61: Charlene Phillips
- *Santa Popcorn Packets* design, page 67: Susan Fouts
- *Holiday Basket Ensemble* cross stitch design, page 71, and *Cross-Stitched Bread Cover* design, page 89: Deborah A. Lambein
- *Cross-Stitched Tags*, page 74: Jamie Leigh
- *Cross-Stitched Dough Cans* design, page 91: Holly DeFount

Thanks also go to Debbie Rowley and Cynthia Sanders, who assisted in making and testing projects in this book.